VINTAGE

LIVING
TEXTS

THE ESSENTIAL
GUIDE TO
CONTEMPORARY
LITERATURE

John Fowles

SERIES EDITORS
Jonathan Noakes
and
Margaret Reynolds

Also available in Vintage Living Texts

Marginal figures
Debates of the vic period

VINTAGE
LIVING
TEXTS

John Fowles

THE ESSENTIAL GUIDE
TO CONTEMPORARY
LITERATURE

The Collector

The Magus

The French Lieutenant's Woman

V

VINTAGE

Published by Vintage 2003

2 4 6 8 10 9 7 5 3 1

First published in Great Britain in 2003 by Vintage
Random House, 20 Vauxhall Bridge Road,
London SW1V 2SA

Random House Australia (Pty) Limited
20 Alfred Street, Milsons Point, Sydney,
New South Wales 2061, Australia

Random House New Zealand Limited
18 Poland Road, Glenfield,
Auckland 10, New Zealand

Random House (Pty) Limited
Endulini, 5A Jubilee Road, Parktown 2193, South Africa

The Random House Group Limited Reg. No. 954009
www.randomhouse.co.uk

A CIP catalogue record for this book is available from the British Library

ISBN 0 09 9460882

Papers used by Random House are natural, recyclable products made from
wood grown in sustainable forests. The manufacturing processes conform to
the environmental regulations of the country of origin

Typeset by Palimpsest Book Production Limited, Polmont, Stirlingshire

Printed and bound in Great Britain by
Bookmarque Ltd, Croydon, Surrey

CONTENTS

VINTAGE LIVING TEXTS: PREFACE

JOHN FOWLES

VINTAGE LIVING TEXTS

The Collector

The Magus

The French Lieutenant's Woman

VINTAGE LIVING TEXTS: REFERENCE

Acknowledgements

We owe grateful thanks to all at Random House. Most of all our debt is to Rachel Cugnoni and her team at Vintage – especially Ali Reynolds – Jason Arthur, Liz Foley, Katherine Fry, and Jack Murphy, who have given us generous and unfailing support. Thanks also to Caroline Michel, Marcella Edwards, Louisa Joyner, Philippa Brewster and Georgina Capel, Michael Meredith, Angela Leighton, Harriet Marland, to all our colleagues and friends, and to our partners and families. We would also like to thank the teachers and students at schools and colleges around the country who have taken part in our trialling process, and who have responded so readily and warmly to our requests for advice. Above all, our grateful thanks to John Fowles for his work. And to both John and Sarah Fowles, our gratitude for their generosity and kindness.

VINTAGE
LIVING
TEXTS

Preface

About this series

Vintage Living Texts: The Essential Guide to Contemporary Literature is a new concept in reading guides. Our aim is to provide readers of all kinds with an intelligent and accessible introduction to key works of contemporary literature. Each guide suggests techniques for reading important contemporary novels, and offers a variety of back-up materials that will give you ways into the text – without ever telling you what to think.

Content

All the books reproduce an extensive interview with the author, conducted exclusively for this series. This is not to say that we believe that the author's word is law. Of course it isn't. Once his or her book has gone out into the world they become simply yet another – if singularly competent – reader. This series recognises that an author's contribution may be valuable, and intriguing, but it puts the reader in control.

Every title in the series is author-focused and covers at least three of their novels, along with relevant biographical, bibliographical, contextual and comparative material.

How to use this series

In the reading activities that make up the core of each book you will see that you are asked to do two things. One comes from the text; that is, we suggest what you should focus on, whether it's a theme, the language or the narrative method. The other concentrates on your own response. We want you to think about how you are reading and what skills you are bringing to bear in doing that reading. So this part is very much about you, the reader.

The point is that there are many ways of responding to a text. You could concentrate on the methods you might use to compare this text with others. In that case, look for the sections headed 'Compare'. Or you might want to do something more individual, and analyse how you are reacting to a text and what it means to you, in which case, pick out the approaches labelled 'Imagine' or 'Ask yourself'.

Of course, it may well be that you are reading these texts for an examination. In that case you will have to go for the more traditional methods of literary criticism and look for the responses that tell you to 'Discuss' or 'Analyse'. Whichever level you (or your students) are at, you will find that there is something here for everyone. However, we're not suggesting that you stick solely to the approaches we offer, or that you tackle all of the exercises laid out here. Choose whatever most interests you, or whatever best suits your purposes.

Who are these books for?

Students will find that these guides are like a good teacher. They introduce the life and work of the author, set each novel in its context, explain key ideas and literary critical terms as they arise, suggest comparative exercises in a number of media, and ask focused questions to encourage a well-informed, analytical approach to reading the novels in a way that is rigorous, but still entertaining.

Teachers will find in this series a rich source of ideas for teaching contemporary novels and their contexts, particularly at AS, A and undergraduate level. The exercises on each text have been tailored to meet the various assessment objectives laid down in the subject criteria for GCE AS, GCE A level and the International Baccalaureate in English Literature, and are explained in such a way that they can be easily selected and fitted into a lesson plan. Given the diversity of ways that the awarding bodies have devised their specifications to meet these assessment objectives, a wide range of exercises is offered. We've had fun devising the plans, and we hope they'll be fun for you when you come to teach with them.

And if you are neither a teacher nor a student of contemporary literature, but someone reading for your own pleasure? Well, if you've ever wanted someone to introduce you to a novelist's work in a way that will let you trust your own judgement and read more confidently, then this guide is also for you.

Whoever you are, we hope that you will enjoy using these books and that they will send you back to the novels to find new pleasures.

All page references to *The Collector*, *The Magus* and *The French Lieutenant's Woman* in this text refer to the Vintage editions.

John Fowles

Introduction

In 1977 John Fowles published his own translation of a French novel written in 1824 by Claire de Duras. *Ourika* was a story that Fowles had known and loved for many years and he quoted a phrase from the book in his 'Notes on an Unfinished Novel' (1969): 'Various things have long made me feel an exile in England. Some years ago I came across a sentence in an obscure French novel, "Ideas are the only motherland." Ever since I have kept it as the most succinct summary I know of what I believe.'

This reference suggests several elements that are typical of the unique and lucid ways in which Fowles's fiction – and his approach to fiction – works. It is a novel in French that intrigues him; it is a 'motherland' that he dreams of, yet also a home that is made up of 'ideas'; and it is the image of exile, or difference, or estrangement, that creates the necessary conditions for writing and for thinking.

Fowles is foremost among contemporary novelists, and the first among those whose experimental work has recently marked and enhanced the tradition of the novel in English. In the 1960s, when Fowles began publishing, his work was markedly different from that of any other writer at the time.

In some ways he was the first 'postmodernist', exploiting the possibilities of fiction offered by techniques that have since been theorised as 'fragmentation', 'bricolage', 'metafiction' and 'self-reflexivity'. He was an exile in his own time.

Today, Fowles may not literally be 'in exile', but he has, since 1965, elected to live in an internalised exile. By choosing to settle in Lyme Regis in Dorset, Fowles situates himself in what he has described as 'a kind of exile': 'I have very little social contact with anybody. The old idea of exile for an English writer was to go to the Mediterranean. To do what Durrell has done, or Lawrence did. For me, the best place to be in exile, in a strange kind of way, is in a town like this, in England, because novelists have to live in some sort of exile. I also believe that – more than other kinds of writers – they have to keep in touch with their native culture, linguistically, psychologically, and in many other ways. If it sounds paradoxical, it feels paradoxical. I've opted out of the one country I mustn't leave. I live in England but partly in the way one might live abroad.'

Everything in Fowles's work leads back to this need for a different viewpoint. It is as if Fowles has to conduct all his analyses by creating separate spaces, or islands, which offer an alien ground from which he can conduct his experiments with literature, with man's relation to the natural world, with politics and power, with moral imperatives and personal freedom. He writes about this in a book called *Islands*, published in 1978. 'I have always thought of my own novels as islands, or as islanded. I remember being forcibly struck . . . by the structural and emotional correspondences between visiting different islands and any fictional text: the alternation of duller passages . . . the separate island quality of other key events and confrontations – an insight, the notions of island in the sea of story.'

If you look at the interview with Fowles published in this

guide, you will see that he mentions his fondness for islands, and the meanings that can be attached to the idea of the island. It functions as a discrete, contained world, but one which can offer a perspective on other, different, worlds. So it is that Nicholas Urfe in *The Magus* can learn about what happened to him in London only while he is on the island of Phraxos. So it is that Charles Smithson is 'islanded' in Lyme Regis – or even more specifically on Ware Commons or the Undercliff – and from this place can learn to see his own life. You will also see in the interview how often Fowles refers to doubleness, or ambivalence, as something that inspires and intrigues him. He likes the idea of twins; he thinks in French as well as his native English; he writes a pastiche nineteenth-century novel with an internalised authorial voice from the twentieth century. As he says here – and has said elsewhere – he is 'a great believer in having the alternative view of all life. That does interest me. I think it's very important, really, to think the opposite of whatever you were thinking . . . If you don't know the answer to a problem think the exact opposite and work out if that works.'

If exile and difference are key terms for Fowles, another – closely related – is the concept of loss. The two years that Fowles spent living and teaching on the island of Spetsai in Greece were formative, not just because they gave him the setting and the germ of *The Magus*, but because they gave him an idealised land of delight that would always be perfect, because it would always be lost. He wrote of the period of his leaving Greece: 'It was agony . . . I thought I'd never get over having left. I had not then realised that loss is essential for the novelist, immensely fertile for his books, however painful to his private being.' Again, the personal statements and the literary philosophy come together. And even a glance over the books Fowles names as his favourites suggests the same set of terms: Henri Alain-Fournier's famous story of a lost *domaine*, *Les Grands Meaulnes*; Daniel Defoe's parable of loss, of the island, of survival, *Robinson Crusoe*; Heraclitus's philosophy of isolation; Charles Dickens's novel of sadness and failure, *Great Expectations*.

Loss is an important theme for Fowles because it supplies – like the image of exile and the idea of the island – a place from which one can survey the 'other'. Loss implies doubleness. You had something, now you don't. This key patterning is one that governs Fowles's constant and continuing self-examination. After he published *The Collector* in 1963, his next book was not a novel but a set of trenchant philosophical notes on the model of Heraclitus, *The Aristos*. Throughout his life, Fowles has kept journals, and there too he rereads and revises, tempering his version of 'then' with a vision of 'now': 'I have recently been rereading the diaries I kept in the early 1950s, which I hope may one day be published exactly as written – I fear not much to my credit at all, since they seem largely an account of a man in paradise who had wilfully and obstinately blindfolded himself.'

As a result of this doubleness there is a provisional quality in Fowles's work. He recognises that in his introduction to the collection of occasional pieces called *Wormholes*: 'All serious writers are endlessly seeking for the wormholes that will connect them to other planes and worlds. I spasmodically collect old books; I live in an old house; I know the other wormhole only too well; thus the title. I shouldn't like one, in any case, at which I could not smile.'

But if Fowles is smiling, the reader is allowed to smile too. The reader is always part of Fowles's double enterprise, the other half that makes the text possible. It is for this reason that almost all of his novels have more than one ending – the best-known example being *The French Lieutenant's Woman* which has two clear endings, and a third in the possibility that Charles may have married Ernestina after all. Another of his novels, *The Magus*, doesn't have multiple endings, but it does have an unresolved ending. It's up to the reader to decide what happens. Just as it's up to the reader to unpick the double stories in Frederick's narrative against Miranda's in *The Collector*, or Nicholas's experiences against Conchis's *masque* in *The Magus*, or Charles's story against Fowles's intruding narrative voice in *The French Lieutenant's Woman*.

If all this seems too shifting, too volatile and dreamlike, then maybe it should. Fowles's novels often begin with a dream. And often it is a dream about a woman. This is not surprising given that Fowles himself has said that 'my female characters tend to dominate the male. I see man as a kind of artifice, and woman as a kind of reality. The one is cold idea, the other is warm fact.'

Here is his own account of the origins of *The French Lieutenant's Woman*.

It started as a visual image. A woman stands at the end of a deserted quay and stares out to sea. That was all. This image rose in my mind one morning when I was still in bed half asleep. It corresponded to no actual incident in my life (or in art) that I can recall, though I have for many years collected obscure books and forgotten prints, all sorts of flotsam and jetsam from the last two or three centuries, relics of past lives – and I suppose this leaves me with a sort of dense hinterland from which such images percolate down to the coast of consciousness.

These mythopoeic 'stills' (they seem almost always static) float into my mind very often. I ignore them, since that is the best way of finding out whether they really are the door into a new world.

So I ignored this image; but it recurred. Imperceptibly it stopped coming to me. I began deliberately to recall it and to try to analyse and hypothesize why it held some sort of imminent power. It was obviously mysterious . . . I began to fall in love with her. Or with her stance. I didn't know which.

This – not literally – pregnant female image came at a time when I was already halfway through another novel and had, still have, three or four others planned to follow it. It was an interference, but of such power that it soon came to make the previously planned work seem the intrusive element in my life. This accident of inspiration has to be allowed for in writing, both in the work one is on (in unplanned development of character, unintended incidents, and so on) and in one's works as a whole. Follow the accident, fear the fixed plan – that is the rule.

We began with Fowles's quoting another (not literally) pregnant female, Claire de Duras. In fact, he misquoted her, but his freely interpretative version of her words is crucially revealing. What Duras actually wrote – as Fowles explains in a footnote to his essay 'Notes on an Unfinished Novel' – was 'L'opinion est comme une patrie'. A 1995 translation for the Modern Languages Association of America translated this as 'A view of life is like a motherland' – rather different from Fowles's own rendering, 'Ideas are the only motherland'.

If there is one thing that holds all Fowles's novels and ideas together it is that 'motherland'. A home, a lost *domaine*, a place from which one is exiled, a scene of origin to which one can never return. Except that the motherland is, paradoxically, also always there, in dreams, in imagination and in fiction.

Interview with John Fowles

Lyme Regis: 21 August 2002

MR: *The Collector* is your first *published* novel, but in fact it wasn't your first book, was it? You'd already worked on *The Magus* for some time beforehand?

JF: Well, this is always difficult. All my life I'd felt like writing novels, and I'd written several before then. *The Magus* used up all my life for twenty years, and I used to lie awake at night thinking about what I should say.

MR: How many different versions were there?

JF: Do you know, I cannot remember now. When I got into the book I used to rewrite it almost every day.

MR: Did *The Magus* end up being such a big novel because you were working on it for such a long time?

JF: It became a long novel, yes. And I can remember the reaction of my poor publisher . . . I was afraid of going in with this huge manuscript, but it worked out.

MR: Why did you decide to revise it in 1976?

JF: Because, like most of my work, I realised it had only been half done. There were many things that I hadn't really said, that needed to be said again. It's partly a confusion over what one is creating. One's not quite sure what one is doing.

MR: Does that mean you were creating yourself as a writer at the same time as you were creating these books?

JF: Yes. That's a good way of putting it. I wrote books primarily to discover what I am. Where I am. Certainly that was true with *The Magus*.

MR: And how important were dreams and hidden meanings in the creation of *The Magus*?

JF: I think fairly important, yes. I have recorded quite a lot about that which I hope will come out when I publish my journals. They are being published in New York by Knopf and over here in London with Jonathan Cape in 2003. My journals; I think of them as a last novel, the last novel in terms of my own life.

MR: You were going to call the novel 'The Godgame'. Why did you abandon that title?

JF: That was a name I thought of – and nowadays I wish I had called it that. But I didn't. And you can't click your fingers and say, I must have it back and rename it.

MR: Why did you invent this name, 'The Godgame'? Why did it speak to you?

JF: Because I basically wrote *The Magus* in pursuit of the idea that life really is a huge game between us and God, or whatever you choose to take as God.

MR: So how did you come to pick *The Magus* as a title? After the writing of it? Or during?

JF: I can't remember when. I was always very fond of the Greek philosopher Heraclitus, and probably I began to realise that I was treading very much in his footsteps and really it was seeing the word 'magus' [pronounced 'mag' as in 'bag'] – and it's pronounced in a hundred different ways, 'Maygus', 'Margus', 'Madji' – in a way, part of me knew that mysterious titles like that have always had some attraction.

MR: Were you conscious of wanting to draw the readers in by offering them a mysterious title?

JF: Allusions, references . . . they all help draw the reader in.

MR: Your work includes a lot of literary references throughout. You mention Heraclitus, but there are a number of other writers and books that you have acknowledged. Henri Alain-Fournier's *Les Grands Meaulnes*, for instance. What was it about that book that made it so influential for you? Was it nostalgia perhaps, or the sense of a lost world?

JF: That is probably – of modern novels – the one I most like and admire. And I have always liked Alain-Fournier and everything to do with him, and I've got quite a collection of things about him. What particularly interested me was that he became friends with a famous French literary critic and they exchanged a long correspondence which I think is a marvellous textbook for any English novelist trying to write.

MR: There are other references too, especially in *The Magus*. You mention the way that Charles Dickens's *Great Expectations* lies behind your own novel.

JF: Well, for years I was teaching the Cambridge Certificate and I was, in a way, using those skills as a critic and teacher, and criticising the things that I wrote for many years – and that was in a way valuable to me. I'd better say at once that I don't much like Dickens, but I do think *Great Expectations* is a great novel. Partly it's that somewhat aloof, mysterious girl, Estella. I quite like the way the boy-hero suddenly didn't know what he was doing or where he found himself, and, in that sense, it has always been an important mystery novel for me.

MR: *The Magus* is set on a Greek island, which suggests other Greek and Roman travelling stories – the *Odyssey* and maybe the *Aeneid*.

JF: The *Odyssey* is for me the greatest novel ever written, without exception. And I've followed all Greek literature since then.

MR: Were you aware of reworking the *Odyssey* when you were writing *The Magus*?

JF: Not at all, though nowadays they keep saying it's my *Odyssey*, my *Ulysses*.

MR: You have talked about the way you think about God and the individual. You also speak about freedom. What is your idea of freedom?

JF: Well, I think the most important thing in all life really is the gaining of a sense of freedom. Demanding freedom, from whatever milieu you happen to live in. Freedom is very important to me, and I live here in Lyme Regis partly because I know I can be free here. I don't have to obey anyone else's say-so.

MR: You have said that when people ask you, 'What does this mean, what does this book mean?', you have given the reply that it means 'whatever it means to the reader'. Do you really feel happy about that? About letting your books go out into the world on their own terms?

JF: I think so, yes. It's whatever you discover yourself – as I was discovering myself going through the experience, and managing to communicate it to the reader.

MR: And now, as you read your own books, how far do you see yourself as a different person?

JF: I feel enormously different. I have really created myself as a novelist and that's very valuable in life. And I think if you manage to do it well, it gives you a seriousness and significance that – once you've touched it or tasted it – you never forget.

MR: Your narrative technique often has double layers. For instance, in *The French Lieutenant's Woman* you use the nineteenth-century novel form, but also the twentieth-century authorial voice explaining what is going on. Are you conscious of all of these things happening twice over, or of having two layers at work?

JF: Not particularly, though I am a great believer in having the alternative view of all life. That does interest me. I think it's very important, really, to think the opposite of whatever you were thinking. Throughout my life, certain periods of fiction have had great influence on me, especially the beginning of the period of great nineteenth-century novels. Even life abroad, because, you realise, I read French, I even think in French, and I think that that is one of the alternative worlds in which I have a deep belief. Voltaire's *Candide* is my favourite novel. It's one long satire on the world he lives in. Effortlessly, the greatest writer. If you don't know the answer to a problem, think the exact opposite and work out if that works.

MR: Is that partly why you gave *The French Lieutenant's Woman* two endings?

JF: I think that was partly because I realised as a novelist I was really wasting this novel, I was not exploiting its end in any decent sense. But for me I prefer the 'happy' ending. The novel is about a person discovering freedom. But luckily he bumps into this girl whom he suddenly realises, by the last chapter, is going to be the person who gets him through life. She's the guide, in the Dante sense. Perhaps all strangers are.

MR: There is an authorial voice that interjects to explain what is going on in terms of the processes of the novel. Is this your voice as the author, or just the voice of the narrator?

JF: Well, in some ways it was meant to be me. A great deal has been written about the book, especially in America, and I've read most of that criticism. I'm doing two things really, being both writer and critic. For years I taught English literature, and so I know about all those aspects of life and study. In a way, I think it was important that I really empowered myself to make all the comments on life, such as 'God is dead'. Either that, or else 'He has absconded'.

MR: I am interested in your comments about freedom. You once made a comment to the effect that 'any belief in God is the opposite of a belief in freedom'.

JF: Well, I've been much blamed in the past for liking Heraclitus – Heraclitus was, for me, a very clear seeker of freedom.

MR: In what sense? Political freedom? Personal freedom?

JF: In socialist practical everyday terms. I haven't much time for all the things against socialism now.

MR: Would you describe yourself as an atheist?

JF: I think I am, yes. I'm hesitating because I do slightly change about that, but I think that the one important thing is to reckon that you know which parameters of freedom matter in ordinary life. And one is certainly *not believing* in the person I call Him up there. So I suppose, yes, I am. But my wife tells me I'm not.

MR: But in addition to believing in freedom, do you also believe that there are restrictions on freedom that we should all obey?

JF: I don't think so. Obviously, you could give me an explanation of non-freedom, but I don't think we live in a world that does allow us to achieve freedom. So definitely, politically, I am a socialist. Here in Lyme Regis I have a very big garden that I talk about as my chapel. I saw a rather rare moth on the wall outside only this morning. This is a rare moth which, strangely, appears commonly on Rhodes, and in some way it has managed to migrate all across Europe. A few turn up here every year. That's the focus for a kind of worship, the miracles of nature, that produces a sense of wonder.

MR: Why did you set *The French Lieutenant's Woman* in 1867? Was there a particular reason for the choice of that precise year?

JF: I think I particularly needed to get a sense of space and freedom and, in fact, in all landscapes I must have space, and so I set it far back in order to be able to feel free in the way I handled it and in the technique I used to explain it.

MR: When you wrote *The Aristos* soon after publishing *The Magus*, you said that you had an urge to put all your ideas down on paper. Clearly, you have always been reflective and thoughtful. Why do you have a driving urge to put thoughts down in some form?

JF: In a way, it's having to evacuate in both the medical and the ordinary sense. You have to get rid of everything that has occurred to you and that has happened to you, and then perhaps you wish there were things you hadn't said – you evacuate too much.

MR: Do you ever review ideas you had in the past and reread your own work?

JF: I'm afraid, yes, I do sometimes, perhaps I should say quite often.

MR: Is that a pleasure?

JF: In a way, being a novelist is a very difficult thing. Everyone has told you what your novels mean, and so on. I suppose there's that sort of pleasure in thinking, 'Good girl, yes I did write that.' But no, I wouldn't say it's a pleasure in that you think, 'Oh, I must get back to rereading myself!'

MR: When you look back now over all the novels that you've written is there any one – or more – that sticks in your mind as having given you particular satisfaction?

JF: Well, I think it's *The Magus*, which is the one that was very broadly based on Homer's *Odyssey*. It was very much what I felt and saw about Greece.

MR: So often your work functions as a kind of collage, fragments of other works. Why is the *idea* of collecting important to you?

JF: Well, first of all I have an abhorrence of collecting, especially of collecting nature, because the key thing in my life is natural history, without any doubt at all. I find collecting beautiful things fairly amusing as an interesting hobby on a very simple level. I like any world where one gets used to meeting the beautiful.

MR: How did you develop the character of the narrator, or the first of the two narrators, in *The Collector*?

JF: I think, again, that was a compilation of a lot of vague things I'd learned. Especially the rather stupid language he uses. But that's a difficult question for any writer to answer.

MR: What was the germ of the idea for *The Collector*? Was there a particular incident that sparked it or an idea that set you off?

JF: Well, as a boy, I was rather shy and gauche and I knew that in a perfect world I could just go up to any girl and she'd love me. And I realise that's a very, very dangerous mistake to make. I had a very common dream which was about being locked in a lift – I don't know why it was a lift – with some pretty girl who would gradually realise who I was, and I would learn about myself through her.

MR: What was the public, or the critical, reaction to *The Collector*?

JF: Some people, I think, were shocked by it. Many people didn't understand that what I was getting at was a feature everywhere in English life, a feature particularly of the very left-wing church, a sort of Methodism. It was meant really to be a kind of Methodist horror story.

MR: Many of your characters are either orphans, or don't have real families – they get brought up by aunts or uncles. Why is that?

JF: I have been thinking about that and I don't really know the answer. I suppose it's a terror of finding myself isolated and alone. That is probably why I love islands. Islands have meant a great deal to me all my life. Because they are a strange, locked world apart and you can't really explain why you love them, why you can stand the solitude. I've just read a fascinating book on *Robinson Crusoe*, in which there was a good account of the real Crusoe, Alexander Selkirk, and how he was isolated. But I felt – as a novelist – that I could have done better in painting a picture of Crusoe, or Selkirk, facing up to the fact that he was totally alone. I adore *Robinson Crusoe* – it seems to me one of the very greatest novels we've got in English literature.

MR: That links with the idea of doubleness, and the sense of yourself always inspecting, analysing.

JF: Well, I think I got that from natural history. All my life I have been fascinated by natural history. And I have studied quite enough. Let me give you one example. We had some worthy natural historian here who decided 'right, I shall write a book about the spiders of Lyme Regis', and of course when he did it he got over half wrong . . . Spiders are very difficult to identify, safely and securely. I know that because for years I did study spiders, and spiders in a way have always intrigued me.

MR: And what about fossils?

JF: Well, the good-luck thing in my life was becoming curator of the little museum down the road. And if you get interested in fossils, let me tell you now, you're in trouble, because they are endlessly fascinating and endlessly baffling in a way. Discovering exactly what they are is very difficult with many fossils. You only have to walk on the beach here and somehow you become hooked on the fossils and you have to discover what they are. Being curator of a museum like the one in Lyme Regis was really rather difficult, having to discover what things could be, what they were. That's one reason why I love birds, too. I've followed birds all my life as well. I think they give you this marvellous vista of a totally different universe, a new universe.

MR: In a way, by rewriting the form of the Victorian novel in several of your novels, you were looking at a fossil, a leftover, and making it alive again.

JF: Yes, I was. These days I often think that *I'm* a fossil. Outside, I have a little collection of unimportant fossils that I happen to like, mainly because they are enclosed in a very private, secret world.

MR: Secrets and mystery. These are two words that seem to be very important to you.

JF: I'm a great believer in the only half-known. In fact, in everything that is basically unknown, mysterious, magical. I must admit that I have been very interested in proper magic. The way that – this is because I am a novelist – people manage to fool other people into believing that they are seeing reality, which is exactly what we novelists have to do. We have to trick them and deceive them, against a reality – their reality – that we don't know. We have to make our make-believe reality the true one, if only just for the moment of the novel.

The Collector

IN CLOSE-UP

Reading guides for

THE COLLECTOR

BEFORE YOU BEGIN TO READ . . .
— Read the interview with Fowles. You will see there that he identifies a number of themes:

- Collecting
- Imprisonment and isolation
- Discovering oneself through another
- English, left-wing Methodism
- Double points of view

Other themes and techniques that may be useful to consider while reading the novel include:

- The creation of atmosphere
- Sense of place
- Possession and manipulation
- Social status
- Authenticity

Reading activities: detailed analysis

Focus on: the title

EXPLORE THE CONNOTATIONS . . .

— What connotations does the idea of 'the collector' have for you? Think of an antique collector or an art collector – what notions of connoisseurship and of elitism are associated with these? Now consider a butterfly collector or someone who collects wild animals – how are the ideas of 'knowing' and 'owning' related in this kind of collecting? Do you feel differently about the collecting of dead animals from art collecting? In the interview Fowles – a keen natural historian – says that he has always thought there is something wrong with all forms of collecting. Elsewhere he has said, 'I loathe guns and people who collect living things.' Miranda in this novel later expresses the view that collectors are 'anti-life, anti-art, anti-everything'. Consider and discuss these claims.

Focus on: the epigraph

BEAR IN MIND . . .

— The epigraph is in old French and means 'no one knew about this apart from them'. We will return to this idea when you have reached the end of the novel. For now, bear it in mind as you read the novel, which borrows from medieval French romances, especially in the way it represents the relationship between eroticism and status.

PART I
SECTION 1 (pp. 9–19)

Focus on: the 1960s

CONTEXTUALISE . . .

— *The Collector* was published in 1963. What hints are there in the opening section of the narrative about when it is set? Is it set at the time of its publication? Use the Internet and any other resources available to you (there might be a copy in your local library of the *Chronology of the Twentieth Century*, for instance) to discover what early 1960s England looked and felt like. Which musicians and actors characterise the period? What were the most popular films and television series? How did people dress in the 1960s? What major political events took place? Which important novels were published at this time? Who were the early 1960s icons? The following list suggests some starting points:

- David Bailey
- *Bazaar*
- Mary Quant
- Michael Caine
- The Beatles
- Marianne Faithfull
- Harold Macmillan
- The Profumo affair
- The contraceptive pill
- The 1963 nuclear test-ban treaty

- Robert Fraser
- TV series *The Avengers*

— You might also refer to *Sixties London*, photographs by Dorothy Bohm (1996), or to *Ready, Steady, Go! The Smashing Rise and Giddy Fall of Swinging London* (2002).

Focus on: the narrator

EXAMINE AND INFER . . .
— The first part of the novel (up to p. 113) is narrated by a character who reveals himself in stages and often without realising quite what he is revealing. Although we do not learn his name until p. 39, we can pick up a good deal from his voice, his idiom, his attitudes and his frames of reference. As you read these opening pages, underline all the words and phrases that indicate aspects of the narrator's character, attitudes and education. In particular, what seem to be his attitudes to women and to issues of social status? How does his interest in collecting butterflies relate to these social issues? Consider his habit of watching others from a distance, of keeping records and of making judgements. What prejudices does he reveal? How cultured does he seem to be? In what ways has his life been impoverished – literally and metaphorically? To guide your reading, refer to the exercise on 'the Few and the Many' in the Contexts section (pp. 74–5).

Focus on: articulate and inarticulate protagonists

COMPARE . . .
— Fowles comments on and criticises the glamorisation of the inarticulate. J. D. Salinger's *The Catcher in the Rye* (1951), the novel that Miranda advises Frederick to read (on p. 148), offers a brilliant presentation of an inarticulate narrator.

If you are familiar with Holden Caulfield, the protagonist

in *The Catcher in The Rye*, compare and contrast him with Fowles's narrator in *The Collector*.

Focus on: the confessional narrative

COMPARE . . .

— The narrative reads like a kind of confession, written or spoken after the events it records have finished. The idea of a confessional narrative developed from the epistolary form (a narrative created from an exchange of letters) popular in eighteenth-century novels, such as Samuel Richardson's *Pamela* (1740). Read at least a part of Richardson's novel and compare the epistolary form he employs with the confessional, diary form of narrative in *The Collector*. Alternatively, read the opening of *The Catcher in the Rye*, which shares with *The Collector* the idea of a narrative which reads partly as a confession, partly as a self-justification – possibly to a psychiatrist. In what ways do these narrative forms confer a sense of intimacy with the narrator, of being given privileged access to private thoughts – almost of voyeurism? Ask yourself, as you read this narrative, to whom it is addressed. Is the narrator talking to himself, as in a personal diary? Is it addressed to you, the reader? Or could it be a literal confession to someone else? In other words, what difference does it make to your attitude to the events and characters within a novel if they are written in the form of a diary or of a confession?

Focus on: issues of 'class'

REFER . . .

— It is clear in the opening section that for the narrator social 'class' is a live issue. While Miranda is beautiful, talented, educated and surrounded by friends, the narrator is an inarticulate and nondescript loner. Consider how his resentment, for him, is related to class issues. What seems to be his attitude to Miranda's social class? To that of his own family? How does becoming rich affect his attitudes? Refer to the exercise on 'the Few and the Many' in the Contexts section (pp. 74–5) for some ideas about why social class is a central concern of the novel.

PART I
SECTION 2 (pp. 19–25)

Focus on: the house

CONSIDER THE IMAGERY . . .

— The house that the narrator buys is associated with isolation, with death and decay, with smuggling, with the suppression of Roman Catholics and with a crypt or a cave-like underworld. Consider the connotations of these images. If you have access to a dictionary of symbolism, look up the significance of the symbol of the cave, and note the key ideas.

Focus on: euphemisms and clichés

IDENTIFY AND LINK . . .

— The narrator has a habit of speaking and thinking in euphemisms and clichés. Consider for a moment the way that these figures of speech, which use language in a way that is stale, dead and often misleading, contribute to his characterisation. Pick five expressions from pp. 9–25 that strike you as euphemistic and five that are clichéd, and say what the narrator's use of these idioms indicates about him. In each case, try to link the language he uses with his attitudes and values.

31

Focus on: suggestion

IDENTIFY AND COMMENT . . .

— Fowles is a master of narrative suspense. The narrative strategy he employs at this point in the novel works by suggesting ideas several times before making them explicit. Identify the exact moment when you realised that the narrator planned to abduct and imprison Miranda. When was the idea first suggested, and when was it made explicit? The idea starts as a fantasy: when does the narrator cross the line between indulging a fantasy and creating a reality? Identify also the sentences on pp. 9–23 that hint at horrors to come, and comment on how Fowles uses the reader's anticipation to hook their interest.

Focus on: power

REFLECT . . .

— 'Power corrupts . . . And Money is Power' (p. 24). Most of Fowles's novels are concerned in some way with the uses and abuses of power. The narrator has been empowered by his money, but this is not the only source of his power. His position as voyeur and then stalker gives him an advantage over the unsuspecting Miranda, and her relative physical disadvantage (he calls Miranda 'a little thing' on p. 23) is also stressed. The novel will combine three issues to do with power: the power that a psychopath has over someone who observes normal rules of behaviour; the physical power that men can exert over women; and the social power that the conformist 'many' can exert over the individualist 'few'. How have these three themes been foregrounded in the novel so far?

PART I
SECTION 3 (pp. 25–31)

Focus on: delusion

ANALYSE THE IRONY . . .
— Look at these statements:

- 'It was a good day's work' (p. 25).
- 'I knew it was for the best in the end' (p. 29).
- 'It looked very snug and cosy' (p. 29).
- 'She was my guest at last and that was all I cared about' (p. 30).
- 'I knew my love was worthy of her' (p. 31).

— Consider how the narrative creates an ironic gap between how the reader views what the narrator is doing and the way that he sees it and describes it. Maintain your awareness of this irony – look out for other examples, and consider how they contribute towards the impression that the narrator suffers from a delusional world view, and that he makes grotesque assumptions that prevent him from seeing clearly.

COMPARE . . .
— You might compare Fowles's portrayal of the narrator's deluded value system with that of Jed Parry in Ian McEwan's *Enduring Love* (1997). Parry suffers from de Clérambault's syndrome, a form of 'erotomania', which causes the delusion that another person is in love with him, and which leads him to stalk that person obsessively. Read Chapter Eleven of *Enduring Love*, a letter that Jed writes to his victim Joe Rose, and consider how McEwan uses Jed's language to convey his deluded world view. Then compare his language with that of the narrator in *The Collector*. Jed would be classed as insane. Is the

33

narrator of *The Collector* insane, or are his delusions within what you consider to be the range of 'normal'?

PART I
SECTION 4 (pp. 31–8)

Focus on: cultural icons

CONSIDER . . .

— On pp. 32–4, the narrator invents a story to explain why he has kidnapped Miranda. The absurd improbability of this story links with a number of remarks he has made earlier in the narrative, such as 'I thought of everything, just like I'd been doing it all my life. Like I'd been a secret agent or a detective' (p. 26); or, 'it was . . . like I had done something very daring, like climbing Everest or doing something in enemy territory' (p. 31). What do these mini narratives indicate about the cultural level at which the narrator's imagination works? Remember that the novel was published in 1963. You might find out about the cult TV series *The Avengers* which started in 1960. The James Bond film *Dr No* was released in 1962.

Focus on: Miranda's voice

CREATE . . .

— Apart from a few guarded remarks designed to assess her captor and her situation, Miranda says very little during these pages. The narrator makes a number of assumptions about what she is thinking, and what her words and actions mean. Remember not to trust this fantasist narrator, however, instead focus on what Miranda is probably thinking.

— Create a diary entry which explains her thoughts and feelings about her capture up to p. 38. Then, if you do not mind pre-empting the narrative sequence, read pp. 117–23, and compare your imaginary diary with the one that Fowles creates for Miranda.

PART I
SECTION 5 (pp. 38–44)

Focus on: respect

ANALYSE THE IDIOM . . .
— Read the paragraph on p. 38 starting, 'No one will understand'. Analyse the narrator's language here – how wide a vocabulary does he have, and how capable is he of making moral distinctions when talking about sex? Then consider what he means by 'respect', and consider the limitations of his view. Finally, still focusing on this paragraph, ask yourself what values seem to underlie his odd sense of etiquette.

Focus on: truth

DETERMINE . . .
— The narrator tells a number of lies, and believes that Miranda lies to him. Pick out the different versions of 'lies' that you are given in this section. What does the narrator regard as 'lying'? How does he identify Miranda's subterfuges? Work out the versions of the truth and of the lies that this section presents to you.

ASSESS . . .
— How does your attitude to the narrative change once you realise that the narrator is delusional, the victim of neurotic or even psychotic fantasies? Ask yourself what role truth plays in storytelling – do we demand absolute truth from fiction? In

what ways do we expect stories to remain constant: what are the internal truths that a text must maintain in order for us to recognise it as a story, as opposed to a lie?

Focus on: names

CONSIDER . . .

— Fowles pays close attention to giving his characters names that 'feel' right. Consider for a moment the possible connotations of the names Frederick Clegg and Miranda Grey. What do these names suggest in terms of social background? Phonetically, what qualities do they have? Miranda means 'one who causes admiration', or 'the wonderful one'. What links do they suggest to other characters, either in literature (Miranda in Shakespeare's *The Tempest*, for instance, trapped by her father on an island and courted by Ferdinand) or in life, either before the novel was written or – for the reader – since then (consider Frederick West, who sexually abused and killed women, for instance)?

Focus on: class

ANALYSE THE LANGUAGE . . .

— Read the brief section on p. 41 that ends 'There was always class between us'. In what ways are the narrator's class, his conformism, and his awareness of the link between class and language reflected in his language in this brief section?

Focus on: power

DISTINGUISH . . .

— 'It gave me a feeling of power' (p. 42). Analyse the ways in which Frederick satisfies his desire for 'a feeling of power' in this section. Then consider the ways in which Miranda exercises power over him in their conversation on pp. 43–4.

Distinguish between the two kinds of power that the characters wield over each other. How are their different kinds of power related to the notion of freedom? Is one kind of power more 'authentic' than another? (You might refer to the Contexts section on p. 75 and to the Glossary for clarification of this term.)

PART I
SECTION 6 (pp. 44–61)

Focus on: silence as power

CONSIDER . . .

— 'The next thing was she wouldn't talk' (p. 45). Miranda retreats into silence a number of times during her captivity. Consider how the idea of silence as a kind of power is developed on pp. 45–6.

Focus on: gender roles

APPLY AND ASSESS . . .

— Fowles has written (in 'Notes on an Unfinished Novel') that 'my female characters tend to dominate the male. I see man as a kind of artifice, and woman as a kind of reality. The one is cold idea, the other is warm fact.' Bring this idea to bear in your reading of *The Collector* up to p. 61 and assess how useful you find it.

Focus on: symbols and gestures

INTERPRET . . .

— When Miranda smashes Frederick's china ducks on p. 54, she is expressing her contempt for everything that, in her eyes, they represent about the attitudes and values of Frederick's

37

social group. Use her statements during this conversation (and before this, too) to interpret exactly what the ducks symbolise in Miranda's eyes, and why she hates those values.

Focus on: *living and dead images*

TRACE AND REFLECT . . .
— Throughout the novel, Miranda is associated with images of life, feeling and freedom, and Frederick is associated with images of death, deadened perception and imprisonment. How are these associations developed on pp. 44–61? In particular, reflect on their discussions about collecting dead butterflies versus appreciating alive nature, about his 'dead' way of speaking (p. 56) and about the value of photography versus that of art.

Focus on: *Caliban*

INVESTIGATE THE ALLUSION . . .
— Frederick has earlier named himself Ferdinand, believing it to sound exotic and distinguished – qualities he knows he lacks. He is apparently unaware that in *The Tempest*, Ferdinand was the royal, handsome, courageous and honourable suitor to the teenage Miranda. Allusions to *The Tempest* recur throughout the novel, and there are some parallels between the texts, although the realism of *The Collector* contrasts with the atmosphere of Shakespeare's romance. At this point in the narrative, Miranda now dubs Frederick 'Caliban', the name of the savage and deformed slave in *The Tempest*, who (according to Prospero, Miranda's father) has tried to rape her. Caliban is intelligent and cunning, and not insensible to beauty, but his physical deformity is loathsome and represents his spiritual inferiority. Miranda is suggesting that Frederick is barely human, but she is also implicitly pointing out her natural and social superiority. She seems to regard Frederick as the epitome of the unenlight-

ened world of mass education and vulgar taste. In what ways has Miranda revealed her belief in her own superiority in the novel so far?

Focus on: photography and painting

EXAMINE THE METAPHORS . . .

— Consider the connotations of 'taking' a photograph and of 'capturing' someone on film. Do the same connotations of stealing and possession apply to painting a portrait? Consider the metaphors that are used for painting: 'expressing', for instance, or 'representing' – both images suggestive of giving out rather than of taking in, of creating rather than capturing. Consider how photography has connotations of voyeurism (think of Frederick taking photographs of couples at the start of the novel): does 'life drawing' have the same connotations? Given the different connotations of photography and of painting, it is fitting that Frederick is a photographer and Miranda an artist. Think about the different ways that they talk about love. He equates love with possession; she equates it with freedom and self-expression. Examine how their attitudes to art are used as metaphors for their attitudes to life and to love.

PART I
SECTION 7 (pp. 61–73)

Focus on: psychological profile

TRANSFORM . . .

— 'I never had any nasty desire to take advantage of the situation,' Frederick claims (p. 62). He is at pains to convince us – or himself? – of his respectful intentions despite the gross disrespect of keeping Miranda a prisoner against her will. Find out what the following psychological terms mean:

- Transference
- Denial
- Repression

— When you have established what these terms mean, turn your attention back to the narrative so far. Can you find examples in Frederick's attitudes to Miranda? Think about how reading the novel in the light of these terms might change your attitude to him. Do you think that he frequently represses his desires? Based on what you have read so far, create a psychoanalytical profile of Frederick.

Focus on: abduction figures

RESEARCH . . .

— Leaving aside Frederick's bizarre statement that more people would abduct strangers if they had the time and the money, consider his claim that 'there's more of it now than anyone knows' (p. 70). What are the abduction figures per annum in England? Try to find out using the Internet. How easy is it to find this information?

Focus on: Frederick's language

RECREATE . . .

— 'You know how rain takes the colour out of everything? That's what you do to the English language' (p. 67). Previously, Miranda has said that Frederick's language is 'suburban, it's stale, it's dead' (p. 56). Look carefully at his clichéd use of idioms and adjectives in this section, then write an incident that would fit into his narrative at this point, imitating his style. You will see that Fowles speaks in the interview about Frederick's language.

PART I
SECTION 8 (pp. 73–89)

Focus on: realism and metaphor

INTERPRET . . .
— Frederick's shallow world view is evident in his bewilderment that Miranda should find her imprisonment so stifling, when he treats her 'with respect' and is willing to buy her anything. The physical images of airlessness, damp, gagging and binding convey the feel of her experience to the reader, however, and these images operate both as a realistic portrayal of physical restriction and as a metaphorical expression of the stifling atmosphere that Frederick's company engenders. What aspects of Frederick's character, conversation and cultural views on pp. 73–7 make his company so stifling to Miranda?

Focus on: Frederick's fragmented mind

APPLY AND INTERPRET . . .
— From the moment that Frederick captures Miranda, he has struggled to reconcile the real person with the ideal that he had worshipped from afar. He continues to try to idealise her, but her verbal attacks, her wit and her unpredictable mood swings bewilder him. If you did the exercise on Frederick's psychoanalytical profile (in Part 1, Section 7, on pp. 39–40), look back and refresh your memory of what transference, denial and repression mean. Use these ideas to attempt an explanation of Frederick's behaviour on pp. 77–89. In particular, read the two paragraphs on pp. 79–80, starting 'When I got home' and finishing 'and then open up', and consider the effects created by the juxtaposition of the contrasting sets of images in these two paragraphs.

Focus on: the Few and the Many

CONTEXTUALISE . . .

— Look closely at Frederick and Miranda's discussion of marriage on pp. 84–5. Read the exercise in the Contexts section on 'the Few and the Many' (pp. 74–5). What light do these ideas throw on their short discussion?

— Consider the validity of the claim that 'the intended social parable in *The Collector* about Clegg's essential innocence – as a victim of poor education – is lost on the reader because the revulsion we feel at his immediate actions eclipses any consideration of their social causes'.

PART I
SECTION 9 (pp. 89–102)

Focus on: sex

WORK OUT AND ANALYSE . . .

— In contrast to Miranda's claim that 'sex is just an activity, like anything else' (p. 101), Frederick has a strangely complicated attitude to sex. Using this section, find examples to illustrate his attitude to sex, and try to analyse it. For instance, his need to repress his sexual feelings for Miranda seems to undergo a transformation during this scene, from idealising her as a sexless goddess, into transferring his disgust at his own sexuality to her and calling her a prostitute. If you did the exercise on transference, denial and repression in Part 1, Section 7, on pp. 39–40, it might help to look back to the notes you made to refresh your memory.

Focus on: the image of 'the collector'

LINK AND DISCUSS . . .

● 'I didn't think that you were that sort' (p. 94).
● 'I know what I am . . . Not the sort you like' (p. 97).

— What does Frederick mean by 'the sort' in both of these instances? What attitudes to sex are betrayed by this phrase? And what does it indicate about how he sees other people? This phrase links Frederick's deadened sensibility and the conventional banality of his values with his identity as a 'collector' who sorts beautiful living things into dead categories. Using this idea as a starting point, discuss the symbolic connotations of the image of 'the collector' that Fowles has used in the novel so far.

Focus on: Miranda

RECREATE . . .
— Retell the events on pp. 96–100 from Miranda's point of view, taking care to give some insight into her intentions, her thoughts and her feelings.

PART I
SECTION 10 (pp. 102–13)

Focus on: decency and obscenity

DISTINGUISH . . .
— Analyse Frederick's reasons for wanting to take more photographs of Miranda. How can this wish be reconciled with the fact that he did not want to have sex with her? In a curiously archaic expression, he claims that her earlier attempt

to seduce him makes her 'no better than a common street-woman' (p. 107), whereas she claims that he's 'breaking every decent human law, every decent human relationship, every decent thing that's ever happened between your sex and mine' (p. 107). Distinguish between his concept of 'decency' and hers.

DEFINE . . .

— By stimulating our revulsion at Frederick's act of photographing Miranda, Fowles sharpens the awareness of our need for beauty and for goodness. What is it about the photographs that he takes on p. 110 and about his enjoyment of them that is so obscene?

Focus on: Frederick

LOOK BACK AND COMPARE . . .

— Has Frederick's character changed since the start of the novel? If you did the exercise on 'the narrator' in Part 1, Section 1, on p. 29, look back to the notes that you made about his character and consider whether he has degenerated, and in what ways.

LOOK FORWARDS AND COMPARE . . .

— How do you imagine Frederick's physical appearance? Write a ten-line description of how you imagine he looks. How clear a picture do you have of him? After you have finished, turn to p. 122 and compare your description with Miranda's. How does yours differ from hers? What is the effect of introducing an account of his appearance at so relatively late a stage in the novel as p. 122?

Focus on: responsibility

RESPOND . . .

— 'It was not my fault' (p. 110). Frederick has disclaimed responsibility for his actions throughout, from 'I went into that coffee-bar, suddenly, I don't know why, like I was drawn in by something else, against my will almost' on p. 17 onwards. Is it a sign of his moral cowardice and his lack of self-awareness that he cannot claim responsibility for his own actions? Or does the novel support his view, in the way that it develops the theme of the importance of social conditioning in shaping the characters' actions? Fowles has said that in *The Collector* 'I tried to show that his evil was largely, perhaps wholly, the result of a bad education, a mean environment, being orphaned; all factors over which he had no control. In short, I tried to establish the virtual innocence of the Many.' See pp. 74–5. How do you respond to Frederick's habit of disclaiming responsibility, and what is your reaction to Fowles's claim about Frederick's 'virtual innocence'?

Looking over Part 1

QUESTIONS FOR DISCUSSION OR ESSAYS

1.   Examine the theme of power and its abuse in Part 1 of *The Collector*.

2.   How does Part 1 of *The Collector* develop the theme of male exploitation of women?

3.   Consider Fowles's use of symbolism in Part 1 of *The Collector*.

4.   '*The Collector* implicitly criticises a society that compounds inequity.' '*The Collector* implicitly supports the notion of the superiority of the few over the many.' Discuss which of these two views of the novel is a more accurate comment on Part 1 in your opinion, and why.

5.   Fowles has said that 'the two perennial incompatibles in the human condition seem to me the desire for personal

freedom and the desire for social equality'. In what ways might this idea be applied to a reading of Part 1 of *The Collector*?

6. Discuss notions of 'decency' as they are developed in Part 1 of *The Collector*.

7. 'Frederick is too abnormal to stand as an emblem of the dull, ordinary Englishman.' Discuss.

8. Examine Frederick's use of the English language, and comment on what it reveals about him as a character.

9. Discuss the novel's treatment of the tension between reality and illusion in Part 1.

10. Consider Fowles's use of symbols in Part 1 of *The Collector*.

PART 2: OCTOBER 14TH?
(pp. 117–20)

Focus on: Miranda

REASSESS . . .

— By this stage in the novel we have already formed a view of Miranda, mediated by Frederick. However, we are aware that he has a very unreal sense of her as an individual, and we have been denied any direct access to her thoughts and feelings until now. If you did the exercise on 'Miranda's voice' in Part 1, Section 4, pp. 34–5, look back and refresh your memory of how you imagined she would think and feel after her capture. Compare your impressions of Miranda from Frederick's narrative with the voice that emerges in this diary entry. Is her voice as you expected? Does anything about it surprise you?

How does her 'inner' voice compare with the voice that Frederick records in their conversations? What effects does Fowles achieve by delaying the revelation of Miranda's inner voice until this stage in the novel?

PART 2: OCTOBER 15TH
(pp. 121–3)

Focus on: points of view

COMPARE . . .
— Look back to pp. 38–41, which record the conversation between Frederick and Miranda about his name and about their relative social class. Compare that passage with this diary entry. For instance, compare his impression, 'I felt like a cruel king' (p. 40), with her impression of him. And compare what Miranda tells Frederick (renamed as Ferdinand) about hating 'snobbism' with what she says about his class and background in the diary. What does this comparison indicate about how Fowles is using points of view in these two narratives?

Focus on: collectors

ASK YOURSELF . . .
— 'They're anti-life, anti-art, anti-everything' (p. 123). Does the novel support G.P.'s claim, in your opinion?

PART 2: OCTOBER 16TH
(pp. 124–8)

Focus on: addresser, addressee

COMPARE . . .

— Miranda tries addressing her diary to her sister Minny. Who is a diary really written for? Compare Miranda's use of the diary to confide her private thoughts with that of Celie in Alice Walker's *The Color Purple* (1983), who initially writes to 'God' because she has no one else to write to. Miranda has already said that she does not believe in God. Who is her diary to? Is her diary to be read as a secret one-sided conversation with her closest confidante, or as a self-reflection?

Focus on: the Few and the Many

REFLECT . . .

— What does Miranda mean by 'The hateful tyranny of weak people' (p. 127)? Within the terms of the novel, is Frederick a representative of an entire class of ordinary people, or is he more fit for psychiatric diagnosis than for social analysis? As Fowles's social theme becomes more pronounced, do you think that the novel successfully conveys the idea that 'The ordinary man is the curse of civilization' (p. 127)? See the exercise on 'the Few and the Many' in the Contexts section (pp. 74–5) for a fuller account of Fowles's own commentary on this theme. Note that Fowles's later novels portray the theme of his protagonists struggling in some way against the tyranny of the weak, the ordinary and the conventional, especially when this tyranny expresses itself as the enslaving power of fear in their own minds.

PART 2: OCTOBER 17TH AND 18TH
(pp. 129–36)

Focus on: Miranda

INTERPRET . . .

— Fowles has described Miranda as 'a prig, a liberal-humanist snob'. Do those qualities show themselves in this diary entry, and if so, how?

Focus on: feeling and believing

ASSESS . . .

— 'The only thing that really matters is feeling and living what you believe – so long as it's something more than belief in your own comfort' (p. 135). What do you think of Miranda's maxim? Is it a useful model for political debate? Miranda has scripted this diary entry into the debate she would like to have had with Frederick: it satisfies her idea of a good argument, well said. Is it a good argument, in your opinion? Within the terms of the novel, what value is placed upon feeling and believing?

PART 2: OCTOBER 19TH
(pp. 137–40)

Focus on: nature

COMPARE . . .

— Compare Miranda's description of being in the garden at night on p. 137 with Frederick's on pp. 61–2. Contrast their different attitudes to the night air.

49

Focus on: familiarity

COMMENT . . .
— 'We're like two people who've been married years' (p. 140).
How do you react to this image of marriage? Is Miranda commenting on the deadening effect of conventional values?

PART 2: OCTOBER 20TH
(pp. 141–6)

Focus on: G.P.

COMPARE AND CONTRAST . . .
— Read Miranda's thoughts on G.P. in this diary entry, including his epigrams on pp. 143–5. Consider why Fowles has included this portrait of his world view and his convictions at this point in the novel. In what ways is G.P.'s world view in opposition to Frederick's? You may find it interesting to compare and contrast G.P.'s *pensées* with Fowles's in the section 'The Importance of Art' in *The Aristos*.

PART 2: OCTOBER 21ST
(pp. 147–50)

Focus on: sympathy

GAUGE YOUR REACTION . . .
— Who do you feel more sympathy for in this diary entry – Frederick or Miranda? Explain why.

Focus on: interpretation

PERFORM . . .

— If you are working in a group, consider performing a conversation between Frederick and Miranda. Either take one of the two scenes in this diary entry, or transform another conversation from the novel into a playscript and perform that. Experiment by acting it out in different ways to see what light this throws on the narrative. For instance, is it possible to manipulate the audience to sympathise with either character by changing *how* the same words are delivered? Or you might try having two extra actors standing near to Frederick and Miranda, giving a running interior monologue: each time a character speaks a line of dialogue, this sub-character expresses what the character is *really* thinking at that moment. How does this exercise alert one to questions of interpretation? The novel gives us first Frederick's interpretation, then Miranda's. Both are partial. How are we, as readers, to interpret these two accounts?

PART 2: OCTOBER 22ND
(pp. 151–6)

Focus on: Caroline's way

INTERPRET . . .

— 'I had to choose. Caroline's way, or his' (p. 152). What is Caroline's way? In *The Aristos* ('The Importance of Art', paragraph 55), Fowles writes: 'Because in general we approach the arts and entertainment from the outside, because we *go* to art, we regard it as external to the main part of our life . . . Even our reading is outside the main occupations of our day; and even the art that is piped into our homes we feel comes from outside. This holding at a distance of art, this constant spectatoring, is thoroughly evil.' Does this idea throw any useful light on Caroline's way? And what, by contrast, is G.P.'s way, at least as Miranda presents it? Why does G.P. appeal to Miranda so much? Is there any way in which the comparison with Caroline does *not* work in his favour?

PART 2: OCTOBER 23RD
(pp. 157–60)

Focus on: Miranda

CONSIDER THE ALLUSION . . .

— 'I *am* Emma Woodhouse' (p. 157). Emma, the eponymous heroine of Jane Austen's 1816 novel, is attractive for her vitality but is completely self-satisfied about both her status and education, even though she has no real intellectual pursuits and is indifferent about using her talents. So certain is she of her infallibility that she makes a series of mistakes that cause suffering to others as well as herself. What does Miranda seem to admire in Emma Woodhouse? Is Fowles having a joke at Miranda's expense?

Focus on: G.P.

DESCRIBE . . .

— Miranda refers to G.P.'s 'fresh-green-shootiness' (p. 160). How do you react to his behaviour towards Miranda recorded in this diary entry? Invent a triple-compound adjective that sums up your impression of his character.

PART 2: OCTOBER 24TH
(pp. 161–4)

Focus on: England

SUMMARISE . . .

— Summarise Miranda's critique of England on pp. 161–2 in your own words. Do you agree with it? What are its limitations?

PART 2: OCTOBER 25TH
(pp. 165–9)

Focus on: framework

DEFINE . . .

— Do you share Miranda's point of view of G.P.? How do you react to and interpret his behaviour in this diary entry? You could react to him from your own values, or you could assess him in the novel's own terms. Does the novel provide a framework within which you can interpret G.P.'s character? He seems to take a stand against banal conventions and for fierce individualism – for 'authenticity' – and he therefore forms a counterpoint to Frederick. His willingness to flout codes of 'decent' social behaviour is another contrast, as are his attitude to women, his sexual experience, and his taste for the exotic. Notice, however, that he parallels Frederick as well as contrasts with him: Miranda is dominated in both cases by a man who is more powerful than herself, both men bully her and both have a strange notion of 'respect' for her. Miranda's impressionable admiration for G.P. is the ironic counterpoint to her dismissive contempt for Frederick. In terms of the Bluebeard narrative (see the Contexts section on p. 79), G.P. and Frederick

53

are both Bluebeard. Miranda, of course, does not see the parallel between them.

PART 2: OCTOBER 26TH
(pp. 170–1)

Focus on: Miranda

EXAMINE THE CLICHÉS . . .

— Miranda has 'this silly notion about English good looks. Advertisement men' (p. 171). She buys 'sensible' underwear at Marks and Spencer. She calls the lavatory by the fastidious euphemism 'the place' (p. 147). She attended a girls' private school called Ladymont and she has friends called Piers and Antoinette. Her father is a doctor and her relatives play golf. She enjoys charades. She is a moderately talented art student who is attracted to an older man who takes himself too seriously, whiffs of danger and is 'unsuitable'. Is she as much a cliché – as much a product of her social group – as Frederick? If not, why not?

PART 2: OCTOBER 27TH
(p. 172)

Focus on: thought and action

NOTE AND CONSIDER . . .

— The tone of this short entry is brisker, more purposeful than the longer, more introverted thoughts and memories on either side of it. By contrast, it emphasises the dreary tedium and oppression of her captivity, to which Frederick's previous account was oblivious. Consider the notion that the novel equates being a 'thinking' person with passivity.

PART 2: OCTOBER 28TH
(pp. 173–7)

Focus on: G.P. and Frederick

CONSIDER THE PARALLELS . . .
— G.P.'s promiscuous attitude to women is in contrast to Frederick's prudery, but in a deeper sense their attitudes run in parallel. Both are dishonest about their feelings. Both want to control women. And both see women in simple, binary terms, either as innocent or as a 'strumpet' (p. 176). Compare what G.P. says on pp. 174–7 with Frederick's attitudes throughout his narrative (see pp. 64 and 105–7, for instance).

PART 2: OCTOBER 29TH
(pp. 178–81)

Focus on: knowing oneself

QUESTION . . .
— For all her sense of being 'knowing' compared to Frederick, when faced with G.P. Miranda seems remarkably unclear about her own feelings. What do the stories in this diary entry indicate about how well Miranda knows herself?

Focus on: Frederick's sexuality

EVALUATE . . .
— Miranda thinks that Frederick is not suppressing his sexual desires, because 'There's nothing to suppress' (p. 181). This accords with Frederick's comment on p. 13 that sexual desire is 'some crude animal thing I was born without'. Think back over what you already know of his subsequent behaviour (which the narrative allows you to do by placing events that happened later in time

earlier in the narrative sequence) and decide whether you agree, or whether you see this as evidence of Frederick's repression.

PART 2: OCTOBER 30TH
(pp. 182–8)

Focus on: Aunt Annie's letter

ANALYSE . . .
— Miranda says that Frederick's letter from his Aunt Annie makes her 'want to be sick' because of his aunt's 'nasty mean mind' (p. 186). Read the letter carefully. What does Miranda mean, do you think? Does she mean what she says, or is she just trying to hurt him? Do you agree with her view?

Focus on: fairy tales

REFLECT ON THE SIGNIFICANCE . . .
— Miranda tells the fairy tale of *Beauty and the Beast*. The original story (that dates back at least as far as the 1550s in Straparola's *Piaceveoli Notti*) concerns a beast who lives alone because of his brutishness. He falls in love with a beautiful young woman whom he imprisons in his castle. He tries to behave in a gentlemanly way towards her, and gradually she grows to love him. At the moment when she says 'I love you', he is transformed into a handsome prince. The tale is partly about the inner beauty of the apparently ugly beast that can only be released once he has earned the transformative effect of love. Miranda admits that 'Frederick had more dignity than I did then' (p. 187), and even that she feels close to him, but not surprisingly she cannot offer him love. Reflect on the significance of the inclusion of this mini narrative about the complexities of romantic love. Is it a reminder of the way that *The Collector* borrows from the

form of the Gothic romance, with Miranda cast in the role of the Persecuted Maiden? Note that fairy tales usually end happily after difficulties, and are about how life would turn out if it were to reach the closure the reader desires: *The Collector*, by contrast, has an atmosphere of stark realism and is moving with a sense of inevitability towards a grim end.

PART 2: OCTOBER 31ST
(pp. 189–90)

Focus on: being and feeling

WEIGH UP . . .

— In the second part of this diary entry Miranda attempts to convey something of what it means to *be*, to allow oneself to be fully open to feeling. What other paradigms of life does the novel seem to be setting this one in opposition to? Miranda has several times used the word 'fey' to describe a quality in herself that she would like to leave behind (see, for instance, pp. 132 and 187), and you might like to consider whether this entry on pp. 189–90 isn't fey. Or do you see this as evidence of Miranda's capacity for 'right feeling' – as Fowles has described the quality that his female protagonists embody?

PART 2: NOVEMBER 1ST
(pp. 191–3)

Focus on: genders and generations

ACCOUNT FOR AND COMMENT . . .

— Contrast Miranda's attitude to the gap that separates her from G.P. with her attitude to the gap that separates her from the 'Nielsen woman' (p. 192). Consider the idea that what separates her from the older woman is not age but sexual competition. For all her claims about the supreme importance of living by feelings, how aware is Miranda of her own more mundane feelings?

PART 2: NOVEMBER 2ND
(pp. 194–5)

Focus on: the power game

ANALYSE . . .

— There's a sort of familiarity about the relationship between Frederick and Miranda, and a predictability about the clichéd gender roles that they slip into. Analyse the techniques that each uses in their attempts to exercise power over the other.

PART 2: NOVEMBER 4TH
(pp. 196–200)

Focus on: emotional literacy

DISCUSS . . .

— The private conversation that Miranda has with Minny about men, and Piers in particular, focuses on the importance of emotional literacy in a partner – on the ability to read and to understand feelings. Piers is doubly disabled by his lack of intelligence and his public school education. This discussion extends the theme of Frederick's emotional myopia to Miranda's social group, but keeps it firmly within the notion of 'Englishness'. If you are working in a group, discuss whether you think that it is true that the English – and particularly English men – are emotionally illiterate.

PART 2: NOVEMBER 5TH
(p. 201)

Focus on: Jane Austen

CONSIDER . . .

— In a 1963 interview, Fowles said that, to him, 'any novel that doesn't have something to say on the subject of whether and why the characters are authentic or inauthentic is difficult to take seriously. It is merely an entertainment. A very existentialist novelist, in this sense of defining authenticity, is Jane Austen.' Is it helpful to interpret Miranda as a character who is reaching for authenticity? Refer to the exercise on 'existentialist philosophy and "authenticity"' in the Contexts section (p. 75)

PART 2: NOVEMBER 6TH
(pp. 202–4)

Focus on: narrative technique

ANALYSE . . .

— How does Fowles set up a sense of foreboding in this diary entry – an increasing sense of the inevitability that Frederick will eventually kill Miranda? How important is anticipation for the narrative effect of *The Collector*?

PART 2: NOVEMBER 7TH AND 9TH
(pp. 205–10)

Focus on: the Few and the Many

RESPOND . . .

— Fowles uses Miranda to articulate the central theme of the novel in this passage. Although she has previously been established as a self-satisfied snob, her views are very close to what Fowles has himself said in interviews on the theme of the Few and the Many (consult the Contexts section on pp. 74–5 for some guidance on this), and this passage is the closest the novel comes to pure didacticism. Fowles has been accused of elitism, even of crypto-Fascism; but he has always defended his argument that the Few must resist the deadening effect of the Many. How do *you* respond to the ideas in these pages?

PART 2: NOVEMBER 10TH
(pp. 211–12)

Focus on: imprisonment

EXAMINE THE PARADOX . . .

— Miranda realises that Frederick is the true prisoner between them, trapped in his own stifling and dead world, terrified of his and others' feelings and of what is alive in himself and in others. He is bound by inner chains that he cannot see and is not aware exist. Examine the way that the novel has developed the motif of imprisonment. See also the exercise on 'imprisonment and liberation' in the Contexts section (p. 78).

PART 2: NOVEMBER 12TH
(pp. 213–19)

Focus on: love as a game

ANALYSE . . .

— Miranda admits that she was playing a 'game' with G.P. (p. 217), one that excited her with its 'romance' and 'mystery'. Read the paragraph on p. 216 beginning 'There's no word to say how he said it'. Analyse her diction here. Is she speaking in clichés? Now analyse G.P.'s words to her. In your opinion, is he playing a game with her, or is he speaking 'out of his real self' (p. 216) as she believes?

COMPARE . . .

— Twice in this diary entry Miranda compares her relationship with G.P. to a game of chess. This image has been used before on p. 177, where Miranda says that 'we seemed to communicate through the chessmen, there was something very symbolic about my winning'. Extend your appreciation of chess as a symbol of the 'game' of love by reading the scene in *The Tempest* (Act V, Scene 1) where Ferdinand and Miranda are discovered playing chess. You might also like to look at the section entitled 'A Game of Chess' in T. S. Eliot's *The Waste Land* (1922), which uses chess as a symbol of empty sexual games, and juxtaposes the spiritual sterility of the over-cultured with that of the uneducated. Or you might compare it with the game of Scrabble that Offred plays with the Commander in Chapter 23 of Margaret Atwood's *The Handmaid's Tale* (1985), in which the game offers a way for forbidden sexual expression to take place without the risk that a full expression entails. What does Miranda's use of the chess image imply about how she regards sexual negotiation?

61

Focus on: the ingénue

COMPARE AND ASSESS . . .

— 'I've seen so little of the world' (p. 218). How does Miranda's characterisation as an innocent affect your reading of Part 2 of the novel? You might compare her with other innocent characters/types in fiction, especially in Gothic fiction. (Catherine Morland in Jane Austen's 1818 novel *Northanger Abbey*, for instance.) Miranda wants to transcend ordinary reality, but seems unaware of the traps and illusions that exist even in the most ordinary of circumstances. Compare Miranda with Ophelia in Shakespeare's *Hamlet*: both are innocent victims of male stratagems. How has Fowles employed images of the ingénue straying into dangerous territory in this section?

Focus on: fiction and reality

COMMENT . . .

— What does it suggest about Miranda that she makes sense of her experience through the filter of the lives of fictional characters?

PART 2: NOVEMBER 18TH, 19TH AND 20TH
(pp. 220–5)

Focus on: presence and absence

EXTEND AND DISCUSS . . .

— Miranda resorts to not eating and then to not speaking as her only way of exercising power. Consider the idea of the absence of something becoming a presence: Miranda's absence of power; Frederick's absence of humanity; the absence of an intervening God. As *what is*, these absences acquire a presence.

This paradox ties in with the idea of G.P. being present in Miranda's mind in his absence, and of Miranda's absence from the lives of her family and friends. Extend this idea of presence and absence further, and then consider how the theme informs the novel as a whole.

PART 2: NOVEMBER 21ST AND 22ND
(pp. 226–9)

Focus on: boundaries

CONSIDER AND RELATE . . .

- 'I shall never be the same again' (p. 226).
- 'I am a moral person' (p. 228).

— Consider how these two entries develop the idea of crossing and observing boundaries, and relate this theme to the novel as a whole.

PART 2: NOVEMBER 23RD
(pp. 230–1)

Focus on: the New People

RESPOND . . .

— Read Chapter One of Alan Sillitoe's *Saturday Night and Sunday Morning* (1958). Form your own impressions of Seaton's character, and compare them with Miranda's. Do you find her viewpoint enlightened, or blinkered?

PART 2: NOVEMBER 24TH, 25TH AND 26TH
(pp. 232–5)

Focus on: authenticity

WEIGH UP . . .
— Look closely at the comments in these three diary entries, and consider whether imprisonment has helped Miranda to move closer to her authentic self, or whether it has distorted her perceptions.

PART 2: NOVEMBER 27TH AND 28TH
(pp. 236–40)

Focus on: sex and love

RESEARCH AND APPLY . . .
— 'Sex doesn't matter. Love does' (p. 239). Look at Miranda's attitudes to Frederick and to G.P. in these two diary entries. Find out about the qualities of fairy tales and of the 'Gothic novel', and consider to what extent Miranda's conception of love is rooted in fairy tale or Gothic romance, whereby she sees herself either as the princess redeeming the beast or as the virgin sacrificing herself to the desires of the dangerous male.

PART 2: NOVEMBER 30TH
(pp. 241–3)

Focus on: emotional illiteracy

JUXTAPOSE . . .

— This entry gives Miranda's account of the events that Frederick related on pp. 95–102. He concluded his account with 'She was like all women, she had a one-track mind' (p. 102). Juxtapose his comment with Miranda's account and her feelings about what she has done. Use this comparison to examine the depth of Frederick's emotional illiteracy.

PART 2: DECEMBER IST, 2ND AND 3RD
(pp. 244–9)

Focus on: awakening

RESEARCH . . .

— Miranda has decided that, now that she knows the death-in-life that Frederick represents, she will choose life in all its abundance, which will mean rejecting conventional morality and embracing risk. Miranda's development from complacent doctor's daughter to rebel could be seen as a reflection of the emergence of 1960s counter-culture, which rejected the hypocrisy and superficiality of a materialist industrialised society. Research some of these topics to gain a better understanding of 1960s counter-culture:

- Civil rights
- Women's liberation
- Peace marches
- Sexual freedom

- The beats
- Assemblage art
- Pop art

— Is it valid to see Miranda's awakening in terms of 1960s culture? Is it helpful?

PART 2: DECEMBER 4TH AND 5TH
(pp. 250–1)

Focus on: light and space

CONSIDER THE SYMBOLISM . . .
— Miranda's visions of the life she wants to experience are washed in light. Consider the connotations of light and of dark, of space and of confinement, and consider how these dualities symbolically underscore the whole novel.

PART 2: DECEMBER 6TH
(p. 252)

Focus on: 'got'

INTERPRET . . .
— 'I got nothing if you go' (p. 252). What does Frederick mean by 'got' here? In what senses has he got Miranda? In what senses has he not got her? Relate this remark to his obsession with possession throughout the novel. If she goes, he has himself. What does it mean to say that he is not self-possessed?

PART 2: DECEMBER 7TH
(pp. 253–60)

Focus on: despair

COMPARE . . .
— Compare Miranda's final diary entries with the entries for February 3rd and July 15th 1944 in *The Diary of Anne Frank* (1947) (for some background to this diary, see the Contexts exercise on 'imprisonment and liberation' on p. 78).

Focus on: silence

CONSIDER . . .
— Frederick finishes the narrative, and Miranda's final words are told by him. The end of Part 2 marks Miranda's silence in the novel. Consider the effect created by the absence of her voice from this point.

Looking over Part 2

QUESTIONS FOR DISCUSSION OR ESSAYS
1. How do you react to the character of Miranda? Discuss whether you find her sympathetic, what you find to admire in her, and what to dislike.

2. 'He wants me to hate myself so much that I destroy myself' (p. 254). Comment on the portrayal of hatred in Part 2 of *The Collector*.

3. Consider Miranda's views on the value of 'feeling', and discuss how they fit into the novel's thematic structure.

4. Fowles has described Miranda as 'an existentialist heroine' because she is 'groping for her own authenticity'. Using this

comment as a starting point, investigate the ways in which the novel – within its own terms – portrays Miranda as a heroine.

5. Consider the validity of the claim that Miranda is freer than Frederick.

6. In what senses could Miranda be called 'more powerful' than her captor?

7. Discuss the character of G.P. as he is presented by Miranda. What function does he serve in the development of the novel's themes?

8. What uses does Fowles make of the motif of imprisonment in Part 2 of *The Collector*?

9. 'I see man as a kind of artifice, and woman as a kind of reality' (Fowles). Discuss Part 2 of *The Collector* with reference to this comment.

10. To what effects does Fowles employ the contrast between the articulate and the inarticulate narrators in Parts 1 and 2 of *The Collector*?

PART 3
(pp. 263–77)

Focus on: the novel's structure

ASSESS . . .

— In the first draft of *The Collector*, Clegg's final comments came immediately after the first part of his confession. The idea of holding back Clegg's final comments until the very end was suggested by Fowles's editor at Jonathan Cape. What effects are created by leaving his last comments until after Miranda's narrative?

Focus on: Frederick

ANALYSE . . .

— Frederick explains the various factors that prevented him from getting Miranda the help of a doctor. How are the triviality, cowardice and selfishness of his concerns highlighted?

— Identify the comments which convey Frederick's deadened sensibilities and his paralysis in the face of Miranda's inevitable death, and analyse what they reveal about how he thinks and feels.

— 'I couldn't face the idea of not knowing how she was, of not being able to see her whenever I wanted. I was just like in love with her all over again' (p. 271). What does Frederick mean by 'in love'?

— Miranda says, 'I forgive you' (p. 266), but Frederick does not forgive her 'all the other business' until she is dead (p. 274). What does this contrast reveal about the difference between the two characters?

PART 4
(pp. 281–3)

Focus on: alternative endings

COMPARE . . .

— Frederick imagines one ending, then changes his mind and creates another. Compare the ending he imagined he would create (on pp. 276–7) with the ending he actually creates (pp. 281–3). Which is a better ending in terms of the success of the narrative?

COMPARE AND CONTRAST . . .
— If you have read Fowles's *The French Lieutenant's Woman* you will know that he – more formally – offers two alternative endings to that story. In what ways can you compare the technique as it is employed in the two novels?

Focus on: the epigraph

LOOK BACK . . .
— Look back at the epigraph at the start of the novel which means 'no one knew about this apart from them'. To what extent does this idea go to the heart of how Frederick binds Miranda to him against her will?

Looking over the whole novel

QUESTIONS FOR DISCUSSION OR ESSAYS
1. 'My characters must be credible human beings, even if the circumstances they are in are "incredible"' (Fowles). To what extent do you find the characters in *The Collector* to be psychologically convincing?

2. Consider the relationship between social pressures and an individual's ability to be authentic in *The Collector*.

3. In what ways can *The Collector* be described as a 'realist' novel?

4. 'For all its realism, *The Collector* is essentially a modern version of a medieval romance, which exploits the erotic possibilities of that genre.' Discuss.

5.   Consider Fowles's portrayal of male/female relationships in *The Collector*.

6.   'I know I have one gift, which is for narrative.' To what extent is a 'gift for narrative' evident in *The Collector*?

7.   Some early reviewers classed *The Collector* as a thriller. In what ways does it borrow elements from the thriller form, and in what ways does it have deeper intentions?

8.   What political ideas inform *The Collector*?

9.   Do you see Frederick more as a study in evil nature or as a study in faulty nurture?

10. Examine Fowles's use of symbolism in *The Collector*.

Contexts, comparisons and complementary readings

THE COLLECTOR

These sections suggest contextual and comparative ways of reading these three novels by Fowles. You can put your reading in a social, historical or literary context. You can make comparisons – again, social, literary or historical – with other texts or art works. Or you can choose complementary works (of whatever kind) – that is, art works, literary works, social reportage or facts which in some way illuminate the text by sidelights or interventions which you can make into a telling framework. Some of the suggested contexts are directly connected to the book, in that they will give you precise literary or social frames in which to situate the novel. In turn, these are either related to the period within which the novel is set, or to the time – now – when you are reading it. Some of these examples are designed to suggest books or other texts that may make useful sources for comparison (or for complementary purposes) when you are reading *The Collector*, *The Magus* and *The French Lieutenant's Woman*. Again, they may be related to literary or critical themes, or they may be relevant to social and cultural themes current 'then' or 'now'.

Focus on: Fowles's identity as a young writer

RESEARCH AND READ . . .

— *The Collector* was Fowles's first published novel. He was thirty-six. He published an essay 'I Write Therefore I Am' in 1964, one year after the publication of *The Collector*. Read this essay for insights into Fowles's views of what it meant to be a writer at this early stage of his career.

— For a fuller account of Fowles's 'view on life' during the 1950s and early 1960s – when he was writing *The Collector* and *The Magus* – you might refer to *The Aristos* (1964), which was originally subtitled *A Self-Portrait in Ideas* ('aristos' means the best way to act in a given context). This text is a kind of exis-tentialist treatise, resembling the epigrammatic style of Montaigne or of Blaise Pascal's *Pensées* (1670). Fowles started writing it in 1949 as an undergraduate and developed it during the subsequent decade. He later said that much of it seems very idealistic, but that he still holds with many of the ideas. His decision to publish it knowing that it would be a com-mercial failure, disdaining the advice of those with an eye for the marketplace, demonstrates his commitment to the moral convictions that *The Aristos* expresses.

— Fowles has always been keen to expound his ideas in inter-views. Read a range of the most interesting of these, to gain a clearer understanding of the beliefs and ideas that inform his novels. You might use Dianne L. Vipond, ed., *Conversations with John Fowles* (1999). Having used these contexts to form a clearer impression of Fowles's ideas, ask yourself how useful these interventions are in providing a framework in your reading of Fowles's novels.

Focus on: 'the Few and the Many'

COMPARE AND CONSIDER . . .

— Lying behind *The Collector* is the notion of the opposition of 'the Few and the Many'. Fowles derived this idea from the pre-Socratic philosopher Heraclitus, who distinguished between 'the Few' who were good, intelligent and independent, and 'the Many', who were stupid, ignorant and tractable. Heraclitus suggested that people can choose which group they wished to belong to, but Fowles remarks that which group one belongs to is haphazard, and depends on one's genes and one's environment: 'The proper attitude of the Few to the Many is pity, not arrogance.' In 1968, Fowles wrote:

> My purpose in *The Collector* was to attempt to
> analyse, through a parable, some of the results of
> the historical confrontation 'between the Few and
> the Many' . . . Clegg, the kidnapper, committed the
> evil; but I tried to show that his evil was largely,
> perhaps wholly, the result of a bad education, a
> mean environment, being orphaned; all factors over
> which he had no control. In short, I tried to estab-
> lish the virtual innocence of the Many. Miranda, the
> girl he imprisoned, had very little more control than
> Clegg over what she was: she had well-to-do parents,
> good educational opportunity, inherited aptitude and
> intelligence. That does not mean she was perfect.
> Far from it – she was arrogant in her ideas, a prig, a
> liberal-humanist snob, like so many university
> students. Yet she might have become . . . the kind
> of being humanity so desperately needs.

— Fowles's *The Aristos* takes the idea of 'the Few and the Many' as its principal theme, and states that 'one cause of all crime is maleducation'. Can you see Frederick Clegg as the victim of a deprived upbringing? Or is he too extreme, too abnormal and too insane to act as a representative of 'a miserable . . . suburban world and a miserable social class' (in Miranda's words)?

Focus on: existentialist philosophy and 'authenticity'

RESEARCH AND APPLY . . .

— Fowles was strongly influenced by French existentialist writers while teaching at the University of Poitiers in 1950–1. Early on he said, 'I must use literature as a way of propagating . . . my existentialist view of life.' Find out about the central ideas of French existentialist thought, particularly in the work of Jean-Paul Sartre, Albert Camus and Simone de Beauvoir. Fowles has described existentialism as 'the great individualist philosophy', and its key concept as the 'authenticity' of the individual – which he interprets less as an external moral ideal and more as a person's ability to resist social pressures, to control his or her own life, to exercise free will. 'To live authentically is not giving into the anxieties, not running away from the nauseas, but resolving them in some way.' He has described Miranda Grey as 'an existentialist heroine' because she is 'groping for her own authenticity'. Using this idea as a starting point, consider how existentialist ideas about authentic and inauthentic identities inform the characterisation of *The Collector*.

— More recently, Fowles has tempered his belief in existentialism with an increasing adherence to determinism, the notion that individual choices are determined more by social conditioning than by free will. He sees existentialism as 'a kind of literary metaphor, a wish-fulfilment. I long ago began to doubt whether it had any true philosophical value in many of its assertions about freedom.'

Focus on: having and being

READ FURTHER . . .

— Frederick's obsession with possessing Miranda dramatises a theme that recurs in Fowles's later work: that in contemporary industrialised society, the desire to 'have' has eclipsed the desire to 'be' to such an extent that people no longer know how to live fully and with alive sensibilities. Frederick embodies an extreme form of this confusion of values, in that he mistakes the urge to control for love, which in its pure form is a liberating power, not an imprisoning one. If this theme interests you, you might read further by referring to Erich Fromm's *To have or to be?* (1976) or *The Art of Being* (1993).

Focus on: butterflies

DEEPEN THE ASSOCIATIONS . . .

— Consider the symbolic significance of butterflies. Start by reading this account of a visit to Maidanek, the Nazi concentration camp in Poland, shortly after the Second World War, by psychiatrist Elisabeth Kübler-Ross, from her 1997 memoir, *The Wheel of Life*:

> I walked around in the camp-grounds in disbelief. I asked, 'How can men and women do such things to each other?' Then I got to the barracks. 'How did people, especially mothers and children, survive those weeks and days before their certain deaths?' Inside I saw bare wooden bunks crammed together five-deep. On the walls, people had carved their names, initials and drawings. What implements had they used? Rocks? Their fingernails? I looked more closely and noticed that one image was repeated over and over again.

Butterflies.

They were everywhere I looked. Some were crude. Others were quite detailed. I could not imagine butterflies in horrible places like Maidanek, Buchenwald or Dachau. However, the barracks were full of them. Each barracks I entered. Butterflies. 'Why?' I asked myself. 'Why butterflies?'

Surely they had some special meaning. What? For the next twenty-five years, I asked myself that question.

— Twenty-five years later, she found the answer: the butterflies represented the human soul, freed at death from the misery that imprisonment brings. In Kübler-Ross's memoir, imprisonment at Maidanek becomes an emblem for the human condition, for the experience of life itself. The Greek for butterfly, *psyche*, means 'human soul'. Aeppli wrote that the successive stages of the butterfly's life are 'a metaphor for transformations undergone by our own souls: this is one source of hope that we may one day leave behind our terrestrial prison and ascend into the eternal light of heaven'.

— Now consider how these symbolic associations might deepen your understanding of Frederick as a butterfly collector, who enjoys catching, killing and pinning down specimens so that he can possess them.

Focus on: mythological narratives

RESEARCH AND COMPARE . . .

— By looking in a dictionary, or a collection of stories from Greek mythology, find out about the story of Psyche and Cupid. How many elements in that story can you relate to the themes and images set out in *The Collector*?

Focus on: imprisonment and liberation

COMPARE THEMES AND TECHNIQUES . . .

— For a literary precursor focused on the idea of abduction and imprisonment, read (extracts from) Samuel Richardson's *Clarissa* (1748–9), which shares with *The Collector* the abduction of an attractive woman by a man who desires her and wants to possess her, and the woman's handling of her imprisonment. Compare the ways in which these two novels present this theme, taking into consideration how changes between the eighteenth century and 1963 in relations between men and women and in notions of class have influenced the two narratives.

— Compare Miranda's diary with extracts from *The Diary of Anne Frank* (1947). Anne Frank was a Dutch-Jewish teenager who went into hiding in Amsterdam during the occupation of Holland, along with her family and four others. They spent twenty-five months during the Second World War in 'the Annexe', rooms behind a hidden door in a house on Prisengracht, then an office in Amsterdam. After being betrayed to the Gestapo, Anne, her family and the others living with them were arrested and deported to Nazi concentration camps. In March of 1945, nine months after she was arrested, Anne Frank died of typhus at Bergen-Belsen. She was fifteen.

— You might compare the treatment of imprisonment and liberation in *The Collector* with the treatment of that theme in *The Magus*, in which the struggle is against the paradoxical intention of Conchis to educate Nicholas into an awareness of his own freedom; or with its treatment in *The French Lieutenant's Woman*, in which part of the novel's agenda is liberating the main characters and the reader from the coercions of the text.

Focus on: the traditional Bluebeard narrative

COMPARE . . .

— *The Collector* was partly inspired by Bartók's opera *Bluebeard's Castle*, which provided the image of a man imprisoning women underground. Find out what you can about the story of Bluebeard, and consider the ways in which *The Collector* exploits the gothic aspects of the tale. The image of Bluebeard haunts a number of late twentieth-century texts and films. You might like to look at the title stories in Angela Carter's *The Bloody Chamber* (1979) or Margaret Atwood's *Bluebeard's Egg* (1987).

— For an example which presents parallels with *The Collector*, look at the film *The Piano*, directed by Jane Campion (1993). Two key themes in *The Piano* are female power and female victimhood. The film-maker has inserted the story of Bluebeard into the narrative to reflect and strengthen these two key ideas. Consider the points of comparison: Ada is a disobedient wife who, as a mail-order bride in a foreign country, is largely powerless. Her principal sources of power are her voicelessness, her piano and her daughter. Her husband, who has a tyrant's hold over her, is seen chopping wood with an axe which will come into play later in the narrative. She loves a man whose face is tattooed with a pattern resembling a blue beard. The elements of the Bluebeard story are spread across the two men in the main narrative, rather as they are between Frederick and G.P. in Miranda's story. In both, love is feudalised, and the erotic possibilities of Gothic romance are exploited.

Focus on: literary 'realism'

ASSESS . . .

— Fowles writes 'in terms of strict realism', a technique in the novel that he has defined as 'the attempt to reflect life, both in style and content, as it is seen by the majority; though not necessarily, of course, as it is valued by the majority'. To what effect has Fowles used this technique of 'strict realism' in *The Collector*?

Focus on: political agenda

CONSIDER . . .

— Does the novel have a political agenda, in your opinion? Fowles's political beliefs are Marxist-Socialist. However, his characters are consistently middle class. One of his major themes is the 'middle-class dilemma: have they any surviving function?' Fowles says that inequalities in intelligence, education and social opportunity are a fact of life, and that he uses the middle classes as his subjects because, he says, there is a richness in middle-class lives that is ripe ground for a novelist. He also claims that characters like Miranda are 'the kind humanity so desperately needs'. What does *The Collector* have to say about how class conditioning affects human behaviour, and about the position of the middle class in particular?

Focus on: the 'angry young man'

COMPARE . . .

— The term 'angry young man', which originates from the 1951 autobiography of Leslie Paul, came to be applied to characters in 1950s and 1960s films, drama and prose who were disillusioned and opposed to establishment values and to the bourgeois ethic. For examples, you might look at Jimmy Porter, the protagonist of John Osborne's *Look Back in Anger* (1957), at the working-class hero of Kingsley Amis's *Lucky Jim* (1954), or at the protagonists of Alan Sillitoe's novels *Saturday Night and Sunday Morning* (1958) and *The Loneliness of the Long Distance Runner* (1959) – both of which were made into films. Frederick Clegg has sometimes been described as an 'angry young man' (and Miranda equates him with Sillitoe's Arthur Seaton). However, he embodies many of the snobbish and priggish qualities that angry young men had traditionally attacked, and the very idea of the 'angry young man' was a cliché by the time *The Collector* was published in 1963. Compare Clegg's portrayal with that of one of these earlier protagonists and consider whether applying the same literary 'tag' is illuminating in any way.

Focus on: film adaptation

COMPARE MEDIA . . .

— In 1965, William Wyler directed an adaptation of *The Collector* (from a screenplay by Stanley Mann and John Kohn, assisted by Fowles), starring Samantha Eggar and Terence Stamp. Fowles himself has said that this film was miscast but 'just passable', and would have been much better as a low-budget, black-and-white movie. Watch it and assess for yourself how well the film version has captured the texture of the novel. Copies are available on http://www.fowlesbooks.com/movie.html

ASK YOURSELF . . .

— When the film of *The Collector* was released, the production company offered various advertisement options to the cinemas that were showing the film. One poster showed a picture of Wyler in the act of directing the cast with his hands held up in the air as if he were conducting the performance, Samantha Eggar appeared looking shocked, while Terence Stamp was shown standing with his shoulders hunched and with one hand laid possessively on Samantha Eggar's arm. The caption for this picture read:

IN THE HANDS OF AWARD-WINNER WILLIAM WYLER

. . . Great moments of screen entertainment come to life and new great stars are born. Now these hands have made an exceptional motion picture. It's from the bold best-seller about an innocent young girl who is abducted . . . a young man, not-so-innocent . . . and the nameless terror they live together.

— In your opinion, and based on your reading of the novel, how far does this — admittedly brief — account succeed in summing up the events and complexities of the novel?

The Magus

IN CLOSE-UP

Reading guides for

THE MAGUS

BEFORE YOU BEGIN TO READ . . .
— Read the interview with Fowles. You will see there that he identifies a number of themes:

- Freedom
- Magic
- 'The Godgame'
- The island
- Allusions and intertexuality
- Dreams, mysteries and hidden meanings

Other themes and techniques that may be useful to consider while reading the novel include:

- The creation of atmosphere
- Sense of place
- Performance and manipulation
- The idea of the 'domaine'
- Moral responsibility
- Love

Reading activities: detailed analysis

Focus on: the title

ASK YOURSELF . . .
— What does this title mean? If you don't know what a 'magus' is, look it up. Are you perhaps more familiar with a group of 'maguses', or, more correctly, 'magi'? If so, where from? In what story or stories might they figure?

CONSIDER AND RESEARCH . . .
— Although *The Magus* was the second novel Fowles published, it was in a sense an earlier novel than *The Collector*, since he had reworked it over a period of about ten years before it was first published in 1965. In draft it was entitled 'The Godgame', a title that emphasises the novel's concern with human stages of conception of what God is. The title consciously alludes to Shakespeare's *The Tempest*, which portrays a magus, Prospero, who holds power over the inhabitants of an island. If you have read the play, consider how Prospero might figure as a prototype for Maurice Conchis. As you read on, keep a note of all the references to the play that you encounter and consider their relevance to your reading overall. Just as Prospero, whose 'potent art' is to conjure spirits, has some-

times been interpreted as a portrayal of the dramatist, whose craft is to 'give to airy nothing / A local habitation and a name' (in *A Midsummer Night's Dream*), so the magus in Fowles's novel has sometimes been interpreted as a metaphor for his artistic creator, or for God itself ('Conchis represents the human concept "God", and Urfe stands for Earth – Everyman,' Fowles has said). For another literary presentation of a magus, read *The Diary of a Drug Fiend* (1922), a novel by Aleister Crowley – himself a magus – about a young couple who are captivated by an enigmatic king.

LOOK BACK . . .

— If you look at the interview with Fowles, on pp. 11–14 you will see that he is willing to accept that there are some parallels between himself as novelist and the notion of the magician or 'magus'. Write yourself a list of the ways in which the two roles might be compared. Here are some headings to help you:

● Stage management
● Manipulation of the audience or reader
● Costuming
● Setting
● Lighting
● Character creation

Focus on: the introduction

READ AND ASSESS . . .

— If you are using the Vintage edition of *The Magus*, you will see that there is a Forward by Fowles. Read it. He describes his novel as a reaching after 'myth', 'exploration', 'different worlds' and 'timelessness'. Assess from this Forward what kind of novel you are about to read.

Focus on: names

SURMISE . . .

— Fowles pays close attention to giving his characters names that 'feel' right. Consider what associations the names of the characters may have. The name Alison means 'without madness' in classical Greek, for instance. Why might Nicholas be called 'Nicholas'? His surname is 'Urfe' as in a childish corruption of 'Earth'. So what does that suggest? And what about Lily and Rose? Or June and Julie Holmes?

Focus on: the island setting

REFLECT . . .

— A sense of place is important in all of Fowles's novels. What associations do islands have for you? 'One of the things I like about islands is the contrast between openness and closed-ness. Standing on an island looking out to sea, one has a feeling of openness. But from a distance islands look closed, mysterious.' For a fuller understanding of the symbolic significance of islands, voyages and mazes to Fowles, you might refer to his text *Islands* (1978). Bear in mind the question of the symbolic significance of the island setting as you read on. Fowles discusses some of these implications in the interview p. 20.

Focus on: the epigraph

READ AND ASSESS . . .

— Consider the epigraph to Part 1 of the novel – a quotation from De Sade's *Les Infortunes de la Vertu*. Roughly translated, it reads, 'A debauched man is rarely a pitiable man.' Think about what you feel this may mean. Come back to this quotation when you have read to the end of the book. What might it mean to you at that point? You will see that there are two more quotations from *Les Infortunes de la Vertu* included as epigraphs to Part 2 (p. 65) and Part 3 (p. 567). Put all three together once you have read to the end of the book and consider how the ideas expressed there might illuminate Nicholas's experiences.

PART I

CHAPTERS I AND 2
(pp. 15–20)

Focus on: the opening

ANALYSE . . .
— Fowles has frequently said that his chief skill is in creating narratives that hook the readers and draw them in. How does the opening of this novel do that?

COMPARE . . .
— Much has been made of a comparison that Fowles said he did not recognise until a reader pointed it out to him – that is, with Charles Dickens's *Great Expectations* (1861). Read the opening chapter of Dickens's novel and make a list of the ways in which the presentation of the two protagonists, Pip and Nicholas, may be compared. Use this list of items to help you:

● Names
● Lineage
● Parents
● Schooling
● Setting
● Identity

- Mystery
- Ordinariness

ASK YOURSELF . . .
— Do you like Nicholas, having read these first chapters? Should you like him? Why might you not? Of course, it's not important to 'like' characters in novels. You are only 'making friends with signs' – that is, a character in a novel is not a real entity, but only the representation, or sign, of an imagined entity. All the same, sometimes it is worth asking yourself about your own attitude to a character. Then – more importantly still – asking yourself what technical methods the narrative uses to evoke or stimulate or promote a certain kind of reaction in you as the reader of the text.

PART I

CHAPTERS 3, 4, 5 AND 6
(pp. 21–48)

Focus on: sex

ASSESS . . .
— What do you think of Nicholas's and Alison's attitudes to sex? Now think about attitudes to sex in three specific time frames:

- 1953 – when the novel is set
- 1965 – when the novel was published
- 2002 – when the interview with Fowles was conducted

— What things – in social attitudes, in scientific fact, in bio-logical development, in conventional attitudes – might mean that ideas about sex alter, depending on the particular historical moment?

— Read these three quotations relating to each period listed above. How do they help you to place – and to analyse critically – the way that Nicholas and Alison behave?

1953: 'In my day, I would only have sex with a man if I found him extremely attractive. These days, girls seem to choose them in much the same way as they might choose to suck on a boiled sweet.'

> Mary Wesley (writer, born 1912), *Independent*,
> 'Quote, Unquote', 18 October 1997

1965: 'I can't get no satisfaction / I can't get no girl reaction.'

> Mick Jagger and Keith Richards (rock stars and songwriters, both born 1943), '(I can't get no) Satisfaction' (1965)

2002: 'Love is just a system for getting someone to call you darling after sex.'

> Julian Barnes (novelist, born 1946),
> *Talking it Over* (1991)

Focus on: reference

RESEARCH . . .

— Pick one element from these chapters that is specific to the historical time being described and do some research on it. Examples to choose from might include: Australia in the 1950s (p. 33), abortion (pp. 33–4), Marcel Carné's 1938 film *Quai des Brumes* (p. 34), the bomb (p. 34). Whichever one you choose, relate your collected facts to the action of the novel so far. Later, you will be able to assess how far that particular theme or event or object connects to the themes of the novel as a whole.

Focus on: love

NOTE . . .

— On p. 35 Nicholas notes, retrospectively, that he should have realised that what he felt for Alison as they looked at the Renoirs in the Tate was love. Consider the ways in which this moment is presented. It will become important later on.

PART I

CHAPTERS 7, 8 AND 9
(pp. 48–63)

Focus on: Greece

RELATE . . .

— On p. 39 Nicholas says, 'What Alison was not to know – since I hardly realized it myself – was that I had been deceiving her with another woman during the latter part of September. The woman was Greece.' Now Nicholas arrives in Greece and describes his first reactions – again in similar terms. Look over these chapters and note down the places where Greece appears as a woman, whether she is a desirable but aloof woman, a woman who betrays him, or a woman who is vulnerable and at his mercy.

Focus on: characterisation

CONSIDER AND DECIDE . . .

— Nicholas describes the progress of his first term at the Lord Byron school. How does his self-pity and isolation connect to the picture you already have of him so far? How

93

sympathetic do you feel over a) his efforts at writing poetry, b) his contraction of a sexually transmitted disease, and c) his suicide attempt?

Focus on: love

ASK YOURSELF . . .

— Read over Alison's letters and the accounts of Nicholas's replies as given in these chapters. How would you characterise their relation to one another? You might even ask yourself whose side you are on. (Note: there isn't a right side.)

Looking over Part 1

QUESTIONS FOR DISCUSSION OR ESSAYS

1. Assess the characterisation of Nicholas and Alison as they appear in the novel so far.

2. How effective, in your opinion, is this section as a portrayal of young people in London in the early 1950s?

3. Consider the role played by letters in this early section.

4. What does the image of Greece represent in Part 1?

PART 2

CHAPTERS 10, 11 AND 12
(pp. 67–79)

Focus on: mystery and mysticism

HOW? . . .

— Look over these chapters as Nicholas finds out about the 'waiting room'. Remember that Part 1 ends with the words 'But then the mysteries began' (p. 63). How is the sense of mystery and of a mystical world being created by the scenes offered here?

Focus on: allusions

NOTE AND LOOK UP . . .
— A number of literary allusions appear in these pages. They include Crusoe (pp. 67 and 70), T. S. Eliot's 'Little Gidding' from his *Four Quartets* (p. 69), Auden and Pound (p. 69), and Orestes (p. 77). Find out about these books and characters, these writers and the one painter, and consider how they may fit into the picture being created of Nicholas and his anticipation as he is drawn into 'mystery'.

Focus on: vocabulary

NOTE AND LOOK UP . . .
— In Part 1, the vocabulary used – for the most part – is fairly straightforward, clear and colloquial. From now on, much of the vocabulary used is more arcane or unusual. Underline or jot down any long, foreign or unfamiliar words that you come across. (Words such as 'reverberated', 'empyrean', 'azure', 'stupendously', 'lambent' might appear on your list.) If you don't know what they mean, look them up. If you get interested, then look up the origins and etymology of the word. What is the effect on your reading and understanding of the story of the introduction of these more elaborate and specialised words?

PART 2

CHAPTER 13
(pp. 79–88)

Focus on: characterisation

CONSIDER . . .

— How is the character of Maurice Conchis created in this chapter? List the things you have learned about him. Then shut your eyes and think of five key words to describe him.

Focus on: Prospero

RESEARCH . . .

— Maurice calls himself 'Prospero' in reference to Shakespeare's *The Tempest* (p. 83). If you know the play, consider the ways in which you might be able to make a comparison between Maurice Conchis and Prospero.

Focus on: the elect and hazard

WHY? . . .

— Why do you suppose these two key words are offered to Nicholas? What do you understand by either – or both – of these terms?

PART 2

CHAPTERS 14, 15, 16 AND 17
(pp. 89–111)

Focus on: women

COUNT UP AND CONSIDER . . .

— Several women are mentioned in these chapters, though none of them is present, except Maria. Alison is one. See how many you can count up. Begin with the mysterious owner of the glove (p. 89). Count the book of breasts as one (p. 101). The number may be ten, or eleven, perhaps more. Then consider how many different aspects of – and attitudes to – womanhood or the 'feminine' or female sexuality and identity are presented in these chapters.

Focus on: Greece

CONSIDER . . .

— 'Greece is like a mirror. It makes you suffer. And then you learn' (p. 99). Conchis is talking about Nicholas's own experience – and the experiences that will come to him. But he is also referring to a general cultural concept where Greece figures as the cradle of civilisation. What is your own idea of Greece? Write down a list of ideas that occur to you – no matter how large or small. When you have finished, ask yourself the same question again and consider how the notion of Greece as a 'homeland', and as a place where identity is created, has been constructed in popular culture.

— If you happen not to know Greece – or Greek history – well, then you might like to look at a guide book – *The Rough Guide to Athens* would be a good place to start – or at a book on modern Greece such as Patricia Storace's *Dinner with Persephone* (1996), to see how ideas of what is distinctively Greek about Greece are presented today.

97

PART 2

CHAPTERS 18, 19 AND 20
(pp. 111–31)

Focus on: Greece

LOOK BACK . . .
— Once again, Conchis offers a gnomic statement about Greece and what she stands for: '. . . like so many Greeks she never accepted her exile. That is the cost of being born in the most beautiful and the most cruel country in the world' (p. 112). If you did the exercise on Greece for Chapters 7–9, look back at your notes and add in this new philosophy. How does it relate to your own ideas about Greece?

Focus on: the garden, the domaine and the idyll

RESEARCH AND CONSIDER . . .
— On p. 114, Conchis describes his first meeting with Lily in the garden of the St John's Wood house. Think about – and research – the idea of gardens and their many symbolic meanings. Look up the Garden of Eden. Read Andrew Marvell's poem 'The Garden'. Look up the word 'idyll'. What is its strict dictionary definition? How many idylls traditionally take place in gardens? And why do you suppose that is? If you have read John Fowles's *The French Lieutenant's Woman*, look again at the opening passages of Chapter 10 (pp. 70–5 in the Vintage edition) and compare the idea of the garden – Conchis's 'domaine' – described here.

Focus on: the First World War in modern memory

RESEARCH . . .
— Conchis tells the story of his experiences in the First World

War. In the end, the sum of all his stories will be a short history of the whole of the first half of the twentieth century. But the war, in particular, looms large in modern memory. You might like to do some historical research on this period. *The First World War* by John Keegan (1998) is a clear, detailed study of the political and cultural origins of the war and of the experience of warfare. For historical accounts of the ordinary soldiers' experiences, look at Malcolm Brown's *Tommy Goes to War* (1978) and *The First World War* (1991), which are studies based on letters and diaries written at the time as well as on memories and interviews. Denis Winter's *Death's Men, Soldiers of the Great War* (1979) is a richly detailed account of the experience of war based on letters and diaries as well as on historical data. It has particularly powerful accounts of the experience of 'going over the top'. Another useful historical and factual account is Ian Ousby's *The Road to Verdun: France, Nationalism and the First World War* (2003).

SEARCH . . .

— If possible, visit the exhibits about the First World War at the Imperial War Museum in London. When you return, write notes on the three aspects of the displays that surprised you the most. Describe what they were, and why they interested you.

— If you are reading the novel around the time of early November, watch the commemorations for Remembrance Sunday. What is said about the Great War on this occasion? The main purpose of this day is to remember the dead of all wars in which British and Commonwealth soldiers have fought, but especially those who died in the First World War. What attitude to war do you read in these commemorations?

— Read the chapter 'Persistence and Memory' in Paul Fussell's *The Great War and Modern Memory* (1975).

READ AND COMPARE . . .

— If you are interested in novels that deal with the events of the First World War in more detail, then you might like to look at Sebastian Faulks's *Birdsong* (1993), which includes the experiences of tunnellers; Jennifer Johnstone's *How Many Miles to Babylon* (1974), which explores a friendship put under strain by war; or Pat Barker's trilogy, *Regeneration* (1991), *The Eye in the Door* (1993) and *The Ghost Road* (1995), which mixes fictional characters with real figures such as Siegfried Sassoon, Wilfred Owen and the psychiatrist William Rivers.

— Erich Remarque's *All Quiet on the Western Front* (1929) is an account of the experiences of ordinary German soldiers. For fictional portrayals of the First World War written by those who had experienced trench warfare, you might read A. P. Herbert's *The Secret Battle* (1919), a powerful account of a soldier's battle against himself and his fears; or R. C. Sherriff's *Journey's End* (1929), which similarly deals with the devastating effects of trench warfare on young men's sanity and friendships. For autobiographical accounts of experiences in the First World War, read Robert Graves's *Goodbye to All That* (1929), Siegfried Sassoon's *Memoirs of an Infantry Officer* (1930) or Guy Chapman's *A Passionate Prodigality* (1933).

Focus on: proverbs

THINK ABOUT . . .

— On p. 121, Conchis says that his mother quoted a Greek proverb: 'A dead man cannot be brave.' What is the point of his remark? How do proverbs work? Write down as many as you remember, and assess their potency and purpose. Or else look some up in the *Oxford Dictionary of Proverbs*. Which is your favourite, and why?

PART 2

CHAPTERS 21, 22 AND 23
(pp. 132–47)

Focus on: art, illusion and mystery

IDENTIFY . . .

— Nicholas experiences – or seems to experience – the sounds and smells of the trenches. He seems to see Robert Foulkes. What do you make of these visitations? How is the atmosphere of mystery created in the text? There are at least two literary allusions – to Shakespeare's *The Tempest* (p. 136) and to Henry James's novella *The Turn of the Screw* (p. 141) – as Nicholas tries to make sense of these events. Find out how these particular texts relate to the images and attitudes he is experiencing.

Focus on: fact and fiction

ASSESS . . .

— Conchis says that '*Words are for facts. Not fiction*' (p. 141). What do you suppose he means? And why?

PART 2

CHAPTERS 24, 25, 26 AND 27
(pp. 148–170)

Focus on: Oedipus, Theseus, Ulysses

RESEARCH AND COMPARE . . .

On page 157, Nicholas says: '. . . as I walked there came the strangest feeling . . . of having entered a myth; a knowledge of what it was like physically . . . to have been young and ancient, a Ulysses on his way to meet Circe, a Theseus on his journey to Crete, an Oedipus still searching for his destiny.' Look up the stories of each of these three heroes of Greek legend. Think about how they are presented, and how the women in their lives (in particular, Circe, Ariadne and Jocasta) figure. How does this comparison help you to place Nicholas's concept of his own experiences? And what light does it throw on his idea of Lily?

Focus on: the masque and the performance

LOOK BACK AND RESEARCH . . .

— Nicholas decides that 'All that happened at Bourani was in the nature of a private masque' (p. 165). You are given quite a bit of guidance in the text as to what a 'masque' consists of in terms of the idea of performance – just as Nicholas, too, is given that guidance. But look up the term in a glossary. How does the performance concept connect to the English word 'mask'? Then look at the end of *The Tempest* where Prospero stages a masque to celebrate the wedding of Ferdinand and Miranda. Does that scene help you to place what is going on here? You might also like to look at Derek Jarman's film of *The Tempest* (1979) where the whole play is directed as if it were a magic show – and the ending in particular is updated with a modern 'masque'.

Focus on: dialogue

ASSESS THE LINGUISTIC TECHNIQUE . . .

— Look at the conversation between Nicholas and Lily that we are given on pp. 168–70. Fowles has said that the way in which people spoke at other periods was more modern than we might expect, and that, when writing about the past, he had to archaise the dialogue to make it sound authentic.

Underline or list all the words or phrases that are formal, or quaint, or strange in this dialogue. Then look through the passage and note the moments where Nicholas himself is aware of this technical sleight of hand. Look out for other places where the same method is employed.

PART 2

CHAPTERS 28, 29, 30, 31 AND 32
(pp. 170–203)

Focus on: de Deukans

RESEARCH, COMPARE AND CONSIDER . . .

— The story of the aesthete de Deukans that appears in these chapters has many analogies in literature. You might like to look at Oscar Wilde's *The Picture of Dorian Gray* (1895) for a prototype. Others might be Joris-Karl Huysmans's novel *A rebours* (1884) or Villiers del'Isle Adam's *Axël* (1890), or the opening chapters of Evelyn Waugh's *Brideshead Revisited* (1945). Whether you look at these books or not, consider these elements: the affectation of placing art and artifice over life; the idea of collecting and possessing; the isolation from the world; and the rigid construction of an alternative world. How do any or all of these elements connect to the situation in which Nicholas finds himself?

Focus on: the ancient world

ASSESS . . .

— A 'masque' of Apollo, Diana, nymph and satyr is performed for Nicholas on pp. 180–3. How do you react to this scene? What do you suppose is the purpose of the performance?

Focus on: the society for reason

ASK YOURSELF . . .
— Conchis gives Nicholas a copy of his pamphlet written for the Society for Reason (pp. 189–91). What do you suppose is the purpose of this performance?

Focus on: Lily

ASSESS . . .
— What do you make of Lily so far?

Focus on: Alison

INFER . . .
— Why do you suppose Alison is just about to appear at this very juncture (p. 200)?

PART 2

CHAPTERS 33, 34, 35 AND 36
(pp. 203–40)

Focus on: Lily or Julie

DECIDE . . .
— Over the course of these chapters 'Lily' turns into 'Julie'. Who do you think she is?

Focus on: the hypnosis

REWRITE AND RELATE . . .
— At the end of Chapter 36 (pp. 233–40), Conchis hypnotises Nicholas. Rewrite the account of Nicholas's hypnosis, but from Conchis's point of view. You will, of course, in order to

do this, have to make up your mind as to what you think Conchis is trying to achieve, and the genuineness – or otherwise – of his motives. Once you have written your Conchis version, ask yourself why you have come to the conclusions about him that you have.

Focus on: names

REFLECT . . .
— Names in Fowles novels often have some occult significance – to the author at the very least. Remember now that Maurice Conchis asked Nicholas to pronounce his surname in the 'English way' with a soft 'ch' – that is, as 'Conchis' not 'Conkis'. Why might it be that it is this pronunciation that is preferred? What other English word might be hinted at through (not perfect) assonance?

PART 2

CHAPTERS 37, 38, 39, 40, 41 AND 42
(pp. 240–78)

Focus on: plot structure

INTERPRET . . .
— There are seventy-eight chapters in *The Magus* and some 656 pages. We are now, more or less, in the middle of the book. Why might it be – in metaphorical terms – that this journey with Alison takes place a) at the centre of the novel, b) on the mainland of Greece, and c) on Mount Parnassus?

Focus on: Alison and Nicholas

DECIDE . . .
— What do think happens to Alison and Nicholas's relationship during this trip to Parnassus?

Focus on: love

LOOK BACK AND DECIDE AGAIN . . .
— Nicholas says that he and Alison 'made love' – not sex – by the stream on their way down the mountain (p. 269). Where else have you heard him distinguish between sex and love? Why do you think this is, and why does it matter in terms of the plotting of the novel?

PART 2

CHAPTERS 43, 44, 45, 46 AND 47
(pp. 279–356)

Focus on: letters

COMPARE AND CONTRAST . . .
— Look at Alison's letter on p. 278, and at Nicholas's reply on pp. 279–80. Is his reply – in your opinion – an adequate response?

Focus on: 'The Godgame'

MAKE CONNECTIONS . . .
— On p. 295, Nicholas and Conchis consult the Bible and discuss the existence – or otherwise – of God. How does this discussion relate to the projected title of the novel as a whole? Remember that it was to have been called 'The Godgame'.

Focus on: allusion and reference

LOOK UP AND COMPARE . . .

— These chapters include several references to other works of literature and legend. Among them are Lewis Carroll's *Alice in Wonderland* (p. 281), the Book of Exodus in the Old Testament of the Bible, the essays of Montaigne (p. 304), the ancient Greek play by Aristophanes, *Lysistrata* – which is about the women of Athens opposing a war and refusing sex for their men until peace is settled – (p. 330), Charles Dickens's *Great Expectations* (p. 347), and Adam and the Garden of Eden from the Book of Genesis (p. 356).

— Look up any one of these allusions and consider how it may connect to – and throw some light on – Nicholas's situation.

Focus on: the Seidevarre story

ASK YOURSELF . . .

— Look at the story Conchis tells about his experiences in Scandinavia on pp. 296–309. How do you suppose that this story connects to the others you have heard? In what ways might it be relevant to the 'masque' that Nicholas is witnessing?

Focus on: vocabulary

NOTE AND ANALYSE . . .

— There are a number of strange or unusual words employed in these chapters. Examples might include 'chlorotic' (p. 298), 'obsidian' (p. 301), 'exophthalmic' (p. 304), 'charlatan' (p. 312). If you do not understand any one of these words, look them up in a dictionary. How many others do you notice? What do you think is the purpose of this unusual vocabulary introduced at this point in the novel?

Focus on: possession, past and present

PUT TOGETHER AND IMAGINE . . .

— On p. 311 Conchis says, 'All that is past possesses our present.' If you look back at the quotation from T. S. Eliot's 'Little Gidding' from *Four Quartets* that he had underlined (p. 69), you will see that it indicates a similar sentiment. If you look forward, you will see that Nicholas says to Conchis, 'Thank you . . . For possessing me' (p. 312). If you think about all these things together, what do you imagine that they might mean? What do they add up to?

Focus on: Theseus and Ariadne

LOOK BACK . . .

— We have already come across (at least) one reference to the mythological story of Ariadne and Theseus. Here is another (p. 313). Look again at that story. How do you feel now about the roles played by Theseus? And the roles played by Ariadne? What does the image of the labyrinth contribute to your understanding of the progress of Nicholas's education?

Focus on: mirrors and doubleness

THINK ABOUT . . .

— Alison told Nicholas about a crossword clue that she had seen: 'She's a bit mixed up, but she's the best part of Nicholas.' Work it out. Now Julie tells Nicholas that she and June were supposed to be working for a film company called 'Polymus Films'. Is there an anagram in here too?

CONSIDER THE IMPLICATIONS . . .

— With regard to the mirrors and the doublenesses in anagrams, consider the implications of the fact that June and Julie are twins. Much is made of this in these chapters. Why? Note also that Nicholas thinks increasingly of certain kinds of Restoration and Renaissance dramas where twins figure (p. 314), or where the 'bed trick' (p. 319) figures. Why might this be? What difference does this make to your attitude to a) Nicholas, and b) his idea of women?

Focus on: Caliban

DECIDE AND MAKE UP YOUR OWN MIND FROM YOUR OWN PERSPECTIVE . . .
— On p. 341, we are offered another reference to *The Tempest* and we are told that Conchis has his Caliban – i.e. Joe, who is black. Look over the insulting description of Joe on pp. 352–6. What do you think of this?

Focus on: sex

ASSESS . . .
— We have heard something about Nicholas's sexual relations with Alison. Now, having fantasised about it for some time, Nicholas gets close to Lily/Julie. This (pp. 350–3) is the first of three serious sexual encounters that he will have with her. How does it compare with what went on with Alison?

PART 2

CHAPTERS 48, 49, 50, 51 AND 52
(pp. 356–413)

Focus on: Ariadne and the labyrinth

RESEARCH AND CONSIDER . . .
— If you have not already done so, look up the Greek myth of Ariadne and Theseus. Consider the ways in which the story might be relevant to the events and circumstances played out in *The Magus*. Elements that might be significant include:

● The idea of Theseus as the hero
● Ariadne's thread
● The labyrinth
● The Minotaur
● The tribute of maidens and young men
● Theseus's betrayal of Ariadne in abandoning her
● The island of Naxos
● Bacchus's rescue of Ariadne

Focus on: the letter

COMPARE AND ASSESS . . .
— On pp. 357–8 Nicholas writes a letter to John Leverrier. How truthfully does this letter represent Nicholas's experience and his anxiety?

Focus on: sex

LOOK BACK AND LOOK FORWARD . . .
— Julie and Nicholas's second erotic encounter is presented on pp. 359–71. How does it compare with what has gone before?

Focus on: the German episode

GAUGE THE REALITY . . .
— On pp. 373–81, there is a story of Nicholas's encounter with a group of German soldiers and their prisoners. Nicholas has just decided that he cannot be sceptical: 'I fell under the spell of Conchis the magician again' (p. 376). What do you think is going on here?

Focus on: allusion and reference

LOOK OVER AND RESEARCH . . .
— As always in the *The Magus*, these sections include numerous allusions. Choose any two pages and note down the references, then look them up and consider how they illuminate Nicholas's story or situation. On pp. 392–3, for instance, you will see 'great expectations', the 'Pied Piper', the 'Byzantine world', the Greek 'War of Independence', 'Blondel' and 'Richard Coeur-de-Lion', the 'Hotel Philadelphia', 'Sisyphean piles' of work.

Focus on: documents

ASSESS THE JUXTAPOSITION. . .
— We are given a group of documents at this juncture. Julie's letter on p. 395 and Ann's letter along with the newspaper cutting on pp. 396–8. What is the effect of all these items coming together?

Focus on: experimental theatre

RESEARCH AND COMPARE . . .
— On p. 404, Conchis mentions the playwrights Artaud, Pirandello and Brecht. Find out about the work of any of these writers. What in particular might make their brand of theatre comparable with the shows that Conchis has staged for Nicholas?

PART 2

CHAPTER 53
(pp. 414–35)

Focus on: Eleutheria

NOTE . . .

— If you have not read on, then be warned. This chapter includes graphic descriptions of very difficult and upsetting scenes. Note how you react to these scenes of mutilation.

ASK YOURSELF . . .

— You are told what 'Eleutheria' means. This is the only chapter in the whole novel (of seventy-eight chapters in all) that has a title. Ask yourself, why this title? This is also the only story that Maurice Conchis tells that is supposed to be 'true'. Ask yourself, why this story? If you can, think about the events portrayed here and ask yourself how, and in what ways, they might relate to the experiences that Nicholas has been undergoing.

PART 2

CHAPTERS 54, 55, 56 AND 57
(pp. 435–65)

Focus on: Englishness

THINK ABOUT . . .

— On p. 439, Nicholas suggests to Conchis that his manipulation of him has to do with something in Nicholas's 'English' character, as opposed to Conchis's own Continental and Mediterranean attitudes. Earlier, on p. 412, Nicholas had said that he wanted to see June and Julie because he 'badly needed their warmth, normality, Englishness'. Look over the exercises that you did earlier on Greece (on pp. 93–4 and pp. 97–8 of this guide) and think about the relation between ideas of 'Greekness' and 'Englishness' presented in the novel.

Focus on: 'The Godgame'

ANALYSE . . .

— Nicholas says to Conchis, 'You honestly do think you're God, don't you?' (p. 440). How does this moment relate to the theme of 'The Godgame'?

Focus on: Alison's death

ASSESS . . .

— Nicholas thinks about Alison on p. 441. What do you make of his attitude to her death?

Focus on: disintoxication

SEARCH FOR COMPARISONS . . .

— Conchis announces that the masque is over and that Nicholas is about to undergo a '*désintoxication*' (p. 445). Eventually, he is left in the cave with the 'traces' of the show that has been put on for him – the clues, the remains, the props, which he can now read in a new light. On p. 458, he speaks of reading 'the old man's duplicities' and his 'palimpsest'. He also thinks about Conchis's 'new philosophy' of 'metaphorism' and his saying that '*The masque is only a metaphor*'. Consider the themes of doubleness, ambiguity and deception in the light of these scenes. Search for other words and images that emphasise this element in a) the plot, and b) the text and the novel as a whole.

Focus on: the theme of doubleness

RELATE . . .

— Chapter 57 ends with Barba Vassili, the gateman at the school, coming to tell Nicholas something in Greek. Over the page at the beginning of Chapter 58 his speech is repeated in English (p. 466). Ask yourself how this little scene, its method and content, is connected to the theme of doubleness as it is played out in the novel as a whole. It includes a phrase repeated in Greek and English, a page turn and a chapter shift, and a reference to 'a young lady' – which may mean one of several young ladies.

PART 2

CHAPTERS 58 AND 59
(pp. 466–90)

Focus on: the theme of role playing

ASK YOURSELF . . .

— Do you know what is going on here? Who is playing which role?

Focus on: the Magus

LOOK UP AND APPLY . . .

— If you can find a pack of tarot cards, look at the card which represents 'the magician'. (June mentions the card on p. 477.) In tarot, the magician traditionally represents an entertainer and showman, regarded with suspicion because there is always something going on behind the scenes. The card is associated with individuality and creativity. Consider how this 'magus' relates to the Magus you have encountered in the novel.

Focus on: sex

CONSIDER . . .
— Nicholas and Julie's third sexual encounter takes place on pp. 480–8. Fowles's fiction has been described by one critic as 'orgiastic'. It is a term that Fowles himself uses in *The French Lieutenant's Woman*. Setting aside, as it were, the cheap version of the idea of 'orgy', consider what other things may make the *techniques* of Fowles's fiction susceptible to such a description. Here is a list of terms to help you:

● Repetition
● Seduction
● Multiplicity
● Frustration
● Titillation
● Mystery
● Striptease
● Reversal of expectations

PART 2

CHAPTERS 60, 61, 62, 63, 64 AND 65
(pp. 490–554)

Focus on: the trial

CONTEXTUALISE . . .
— How many 'trials' have taken place in *The Magus* so far? Think of all the different kinds of 'trial' that there may be.

How often has the word been used? How do you now understand the term in the light of what happens in these chapters?

Focus on: *symbols*

CONSIDER AND RESEARCH . . .
— On p. 499, we are introduced to the scene of the trial and the judges and participants. Consider the symbols, including those in their costumes and appearances. What does each of them represent, and how does this symbolic exploitation relate to the terms of the novel as a whole?

Focus on: *the web-centre*

ASK YOURSELF . . .
— 'He was still the master of ceremonies, the man behind it all; at web-centre' (p. 511). How does this statement relate to the themes of the book? Use these words to focus your ideas: web, labyrinth, maze, domaine, spider, thread, clue, weaving, Arachne.

Focus on: *the scapegoat*

LOOK UP . . .
— Lily is selected as a *pharmakos* or 'scapegoat' (p. 514). Look up the strict definition of the term and consider how it relates to the events portrayed here. Where else is the phrase used a) in everyday language, and b) in the Bible?

Focus on: *Polymus Films*

WORK OUT . . .
— Nicholas says that he now realises the anagram in 'Polymus' Films (p. 521). Had you worked it out? What is the anagram? And why is it relevant? How does this wordplay relate back to

Alison's crossword clue about 'She's a bit mixed up, but she's the best part of Nicholas'?

ASSESS THE EFFECTS . . .
— Over pp. 521–7, Polymus Films presents 'The Shameful Truth' and – for the first and only time in this book (with the possible exception of the inset letters that Nicholas sends and receives) – a typographical mode of presentation is used to show the placards of text in the film. What are the effects on your attitude to the film brought about by this method?

Focus on: Othello

COMPARE . . .
— Over pp. 529–31, there are several references to Shakespeare's *Othello*. See how many you can pick out. Disentangle the numerous connections that Nicholas makes, and if you know Shakespeare's play, go on to make as many comparisons between *Othello* and *The Magus* as you can.

Focus on: fragments

RELATE . . .
— In Chapter 65, Nicholas explores the hidden Earth and finds evidence of the various masquerades he has experienced. Work over these, recalling the episodes to which they each relate. How does this scene help you to position Nicholas's story? Is it important that the reader now reviews all these events through fragments and scraps of information?

PART 2

CHAPTERS 66 AND 67
(pp. 554–66)

Focus on: Alison

QUESTION . . .
— Why do you suppose that Nicholas decides to telephone the airline desk at the airport (p. 554)? Are you surprised by what happens on pp. 561–2? Why does it matter that Alison turns out to have a flower name (p. 566)?

Focus on: Conchis

RE-EVALUATE . . .
— While Alison now appears to be alive, Conchis appears to be dead, and long since dead (p. 559). What do you suppose is the point of this reversal?

INTERPRET . . .
— Fowles has said, 'The basic idea that lay behind *The Magus* was that we are all in fact in a Godgame and we're always in close contact with a kind of super-Conchis. This is the very basis of human existence, for me.' How do you interpret Conchis in the light of this comment?

Looking over Part 2

QUESTIONS FOR DISCUSSION OR ESSAYS
1. What is the significance of the idea of the island in Part 2 of *The Magus*?

2. Make a comparison between the events on Phraxos and those in Shakespeare's *The Tempest*.

3.   'All is illusion.' 'Allusion is all.' Which of these statements seems to you a better summary of Part 2 of *The Magus*?

4.   Compare and contrast Lily/Julie's role in Part 2 with that of Alison.

PART 3

CHAPTERS 68, 69 AND 70
(pp. 569–83)

Focus on: the theme of exile

DISCRIMINATE AND DESCRIBE . . .
— Nicholas goes to visit Leverrier in the monastery outside Rome, but he finds out nothing about what happened. What is suggested by this encounter? Why does Nicholas end by deciding that Leverrier has chosen an 'exile'? Now look ahead to Nicholas's thoughts about Greece after he has settled in London at the beginning of Chapter 70 (p. 576). In what ways is Nicholas himself now in exile?

Focus on: Orpheus and Eurydice

RESEARCH . . .
— Look up the story of Orpheus and Eurydice in a dictionary of Greek myths. Robert Graves's retelling gives you the story in full. Then look at p. 575 where Nicholas says 'And what did I care? Why should I go on searching for her?' Once you have the Orpheus story clearly in your mind, consider the ways in which it might parallel Nicholas's story of his relationship to Alison. Why does Nicholas still want to be part of the masque (p. 577)?

Focus on: fragments

NOTE . . .

— Nicholas decides to do some research on the many ideas and themes given to him through Conchis's masque (pp. 577–83). How far does it help you to have this information at this stage? Or does it obscure rather than explain?

PART 3

CHAPTERS 71, 72, 73, 74 AND 75
(pp. 583–631)

Focus on: Lily de Seitas

RESEARCH . . .

— Find the story of Demeter and Persephone in a dictionary of Greek myths. In what ways might Lily de Seitas be playing out the role of Demeter to Alison's (or Lily/Julie's) Persephone? How does this story connect to the story of Orpheus and Eurydice?

PART 3

CHAPTERS 76 AND 77
(pp. 631–45)

Focus on: Kemp and Jojo

ANALYSE AND DECIDE . . .

— In the final chapter of *The French Lieutenant's Woman* the narrative says: 'It is a time-proven rule of the novelist's craft never to introduce any but very minor characters at the end of a book' (p. 440 in the Vintage edition). Fowles actually introduces two fairly important characters towards the end of *The Magus* – Kemp and Jojo. What, in your opinion, is the function of each of them in relation to the themes of the book? And in what ways do they provide a foil for the characters we have met so far?

Focus on: Stonehenge

ASK YOURSELF . . .
— What do you suppose is the point of Nicholas and Jojo's night-time trip to Stonehenge? Why Stonehenge?

PART 3

CHAPTER 78
(pp. 645–56)

Focus on: Orpheus

LOOK BACK . . .
— If you did the exercise on Orpheus that related to Chapters 68, 69 and 70, on p. 119, then look now at the reference to a 'literal, descent into a modern Tartarus' on p. 647. How does this reference contribute to the Orpheus theme?

Focus on: the trial

INTERPRET AND LINK . . .
— On p. 649, Nicholas notices that the porticoes of Cumberland Terrace, in Regent's Park, are adorned with a row of white classical statues. He sees these along with the other people in the park, as 'Other sitters and watchers. Suddenly the peopled park seemed a stage, the whole landscape a

landscape of masquers, spies.' Later on he decides that Alison has deliberately chosen this bench because it makes a stage for the watchers he sees, in the representations of the Olympian gods, and – perhaps – the real watchers behind the blank windows (pp. 652–3 and 654). Who – if anyone – do you suppose is watching this scene? What other scenes in the novel as a whole is it designed to resemble?

Focus on: the conclusion

QUESTION . . .

— 'The last chapter is about achieving authenticity,' Fowles has said. To what extent does Nicholas achieve authenticity by the end of the novel?

Focus on: the Latin epigram

ASSESS THE EFFECTS . . .

— The Latin epigram that Nicholas finishes his narrative with is from a third-century anonymous Latin lyric entitled 'The Vigil of Venus'. It translates as: *Tomorrow let him love, who has never loved; he who has loved, let him love again.* This implies that Alison and Nicholas will get together, without stating it as a certainty. Then again, maybe it doesn't. Compare the openness of this ending with the double ending of *The French Lieutenant's Woman*. Refer to the exercises on existentialism in the Contexts section (pp. 126–7) for a fuller understanding of the philosophical origins of Fowles's interest in open-ended narrative.

— Fowles likes to tell a story about receiving two letters from America, one from a woman who was angry about Fowles's ambiguity, and rude about his use of French and Latin. She wrote, 'I just want one straight answer out of you – did Nicholas and Alison get together in the end?' To which Fowles replied, 'No.' A New York lawyer, who was dying in hospital of cancer, wrote at the same time, 'I have just got one request – please tell me if those two did get together and managed to make it.' To which Fowles replied, 'Yes.' Fowles explains: 'I tell that story because that's how I feel – I don't know the answer.'

Looking over the whole novel

QUESTIONS FOR DISCUSSION OR ESSAYS

1. 'All my novels are about how you achieve that possible – possibly non-existent – freedom.' How apt is this as a summary of what *The Magus* is about?

2. Discuss the theme of self-discovery as it is presented in *The Magus*.

3. 'I like the marvellous only when it is strictly enveloped in reality' (Alain-Fournier). How accurately does this quotation, which Fowles kept by him as he worked on *The Magus*, apply to Fowles's novel?

4. Fowles has described *The Magus* as 'a fable about the relationship between man and his conception of God'. Discuss how helpful you find this description of the novel.

5. Although Fowles describes himself as an atheist, he uses religious imagery throughout many of his novels. What religious motifs does he employ in *The Magus*, and to what effect?

6. 'Writing is a kind of teaching' (Fowles). In what ways might *The Magus* be regarded as a didactic novel?

7. Comment on Fowles's assessment of *The Magus* that it was a failure because 'it tried to do too much'.

8. Discuss the novel's treatment of the tension between reality and illusion.

9. 'Nature is above all for me rich in similes and metaphors of man. It is the poetry to the "prose" of man.' Discuss, with reference to the portrayal of nature in *The Magus*.

10. 'In manipulating others through her sexuality, Lily is guilty of the same failing as she seeks to correct.' Discuss.

11. In what ways is your reading of *The Magus* influenced by the fact that the narrative is written by Nicholas as a sort of confession, presumably many years after the events described?

12. Does *The Magus* illustrate or confound Fowles's claim that what a novelist leaves out of a novel is as important as what he includes?

13. Consider Fowles's use of eroticism in *The Magus*.

14. Examine the motif of the responsible use of power in *The Magus*.

15. 'He said something to me one day. About males and females. How we [men] judge things as objects, and you [women] judge them by their relationships' (p. 653). How far is this distinction between masculine and feminine helpful to an assessment of the themes of the novel as a whole?

Contexts, comparisons and complementary readings

THE MAGUS

These sections suggest contextual and comparative ways of reading these three novels by Fowles. You can put your reading in a social, historical or literary context. You can make comparisons – again, social, literary or historical – with other texts or art works. Or you can choose complementary works (of whatever kind) – that is, art works, literary works, social reportage or facts which in some way illuminate the text by sidelights or interventions which you can make into a telling framework. Some of the suggested contexts are directly connected to the book, in that they will give you precise literary or social frames in which to situate the novel. In turn, these are either related to the period within which the novel is set, or to the time – now – when you are reading it. Some of these examples are designed to suggest books or other texts that may make useful sources for comparison (or for complementary purposes) when you are reading *The Collector*, *The Magus* and *The French Lieutenant's Woman*. Again, they may be related to literary or critical themes, or they may be relevant to social and cultural themes current 'then' or 'now'.

Focus on: 'The Godgame'

ASK YOURSELF . . .

— Fowles has said that for some time he had thought of calling *The Magus* 'The Godgame' and also that he wished he *had* used that title. Towards the end of the book, various characters – including Lily and Rose's mother – use that name for what has happened to Nicholas. Do you think this would have been a better title, or not? Why?

Focus on: revisions

CONSIDER . . .

— Fowles thought the first edition of *The Magus* unsatisfactory for several reasons: he said that it was 'not terribly well written'; it tried to create a myth in language that was inappropriately realistic; it was insufficiently erotic; and it was not very clear in several places. He revised it in a more mythical language, inserting some new scenes and clarifying some aspects. The revised version was first published in 1977 and is the version that is now available. If you are able to get hold of a copy of the first version, it can be interesting to compare the two, especially passages from the central sections which have been substantially revised. What does this process of revision suggest about the question of whether a work of art is ever really finished, or whether it is just left at a particular stage?

Focus on: existentialist philosophy and 'authenticity'

RESEARCH AND APPLY . . .

— Fowles came under the influence of French existentialist writers while teaching at the University of Poitiers in 1950–1.

Early on he said, 'I must use literature as a way of propagating . . . my existentialist view of life.' Latterly, however, he has moved towards determinism (essentially, the belief that all events have a cause, and that in the case of human actions, that cause lies in their conditioning), and has described existentialism as 'a kind of literary metaphor, a wish fulfilment. I long ago began to doubt whether it had any true philosophical value in many of its assertions about freedom.' Find out about the central ideas of French existentialist thought, particularly in the work Jean-Paul Sartre, Albert Camus and Simone de Beauvoir. Fowles has described existentialism as 'the great individualist philosophy', and its key concept as the 'authenticity' of the individual – which he interprets less as an external moral ideal and more as a person's ability to resist social pressures, to control his or her own life, to exercise free will. 'To live authentically is not giving into the anxieties, not running away from the nauseas, but resolving them in some way.' What light does this notion of choosing oneself, of 'authenticity', throw on the characters of Alison and Nicholas in *The Magus*?

READ FURTHER . . .

—— Fowles has said that 'I'd first of all like to be a good poet, then a sound philosopher, then a good novelist. The novel is simply, for me, a way of expressing my view of life.' For a fuller account of Fowles's 'view on life' during the 1950s and early 1960s, when he was writing *The Magus*, you might read *The Aristos* (1964), which was originally subtitled *A Self-Portrait in Ideas*. 'Aristos' means the best way to act in a given context. This text is a kind of existentialist treatise, resembling the epigrammatic style of Montaigne or of Blaise Pascal's *Pensées* (1670). Fowles started writing it in 1949 as an undergraduate and developed it during the subsequent decade. He later said that much of it seems very idealistic, but that he still holds with many of the ideas. His decision to publish it knowing

127

that it would be a commercial failure, disdaining the advice of those with an eye for the marketplace, demonstrates his commitment to the moral convictions that *The Aristos* expresses.

— Fowles has always been direct and outspoken about his ideas in interviews: read a range of the most interesting of these, for instance in Dianne L. Vipond, ed., *Conversations with John Fowles* (1999), to gain a clearer understanding of the beliefs and ideas that inform his novels. Having used these contexts to form a clearer impression of Fowles's ideas, ask yourself how useful these sidelights and interventions are in providing a telling framework in your reading of Fowles's novels.

Focus on: literary 'realism'

ASSESS . . .

— 'I must write in terms of strict realism. I'm a great admirer of Daniel Defoe – what I admire most is his creation of the extremely unusual situation, such as we find in *Robinson Crusoe*, treated . . . honestly in terms of life. I hope this sort of approach will underlie my next novel, the Greek one,' said Fowles in 1963, when he was working on *The Magus*. Fowles has defined realism in the novel as 'the attempt to reflect life, both in style and content, as it is seen by the majority; though not necessarily, of course, as it is valued by the majority. I suppose I mean something like "traditional technique but original vision".' To what extent does this describe the technique Fowles has used in *The Magus*?

Focus on: a secret world, or the idea of the 'domaine'

COMPARE . . .

— Fowles has described the essential idea of *The Magus* as 'a secret world, whose penetration involved ordeal and whose final reward was self-knowledge'. Expressed like this, the plot resembles the archetype of the quest, which has many antecedents dating back to Homer's legends the *Iliad* and the *Odyssey*. 'The notion of the quest has always attracted me very deeply, especially in the early Celtic novels. Another person who's influenced me in a bizarre way is a lady called Marie de France. The whole essence of good fiction writing really is in those very short stories.' Fowles includes in his collection of short stories, *The Ebony Tower* (1974), a translation of Marie de France's twelfth-century romance, *Eliduc*. Other instances of quest narratives include Dickens's *Great Expectations* (1860–1), which Fowles taught while he was writing *The Magus*, and more recently Thomas Pynchon's *The Crying of Lot 49* (1966), which has a protagonist who, in a search of an enigmatic industrialist, finds herself following occult symbols in a bewildering new world. Donna Tartt's 1992 novel *The Secret History* figures a young, aimless protagonist who gets caught up in a mystery with a sinister group of scholars at a New England university. Both of these novels weave classical allusions and themes into their modern plots. Compare the ways in which one or both of these novels employ mystery and a sense of the quest in a confusing world with how Fowles employs these ideas in *The Magus*.

Focus on: allusion and dramatic personae

LIST AND ASSESS . . .

— At various times Nicholas compares himself to different literary and mythological characters including Robinson Crusoe, Alice, Pip in Dickens's *Great Expectations*, Joseph K. in Franz Kafka's *The Trial*, Marlow in Joseph Conrad's *The Heart of Darkness*, Caliban, Hamlet and Orpheus. Look over the novel and see how many more you can find. Which passages and scenes in Nicholas's story most closely relate to the experiences of these fictional characters? Assess what these illusions bring to the narrative.

Focus on: literary precursor

COMPARE . . .

— Le Grand Meaulnes (The Wanderer) by Henri Alain-Fournier (1913) has been an influential novel on Fowles's ideas throughout his life, and The Magus is in a sense a reworking of this novel. Read Le Grand Meaulnes and assess to what extent and in which ways the influence of this novel is evident in The Magus, especially in the treatment of the concept of loss. You might refer to the afterword that Fowles has written to The Wanderer (1971).

Focus on: literary successor

COMPARE . . .

— The eponymous hero of Daniel Martin (1977) is, according to his creator, Nicholas Urfe, as he might be twenty-five years on. Read Fowles's later novel and compare the two characters. Is this comparison helpful?

Focus on: the Bildungsroman

RESEARCH AND DEFINE . . .

— A 'Bildungsroman' is a German term for 'the novel of education'. It is a distinctive literary form that came to prominence in the late eighteenth century and has been popular ever since. Essentially, a young person is 'educated' in life and comes to some understanding of themselves and their own situation as they grow up. Examples might include Jane Austen's *Emma* (1816), Charles Dickens's *David Copperfield* (1849–50), Charlotte Brontë's *Jane Eyre* (1847), F. Scott Fitzgerald's *The Great Gatsby* (1925), Muriel Spark's *The Prime of Miss Jean Brodie* (1961), Alice Walker's *The Color Purple* (1983) and Jeanette Winterson's *Oranges Are Not the Only Fruit* (1985).

— How many other examples can you think of from your own reading? In what ways could you describe *The Magus* as a '*Bildungsroman*'?

Focus on: the feminine principle

CONSIDER AND DISCUSS . . .

— Fowles was influenced by Jung's notion of the 'anima', or feminine principle, an archetype in the collective unconscious which is projected on to experience. He has said that his female characters 'are usually standing for other things. Women enshrine right feeling; a comprehensiveness of reaction to the world. Reason and right feeling are not the same thing.' How helpful do you find these comments in your interpretation of Fowles's female characters?

ASK YOURSELF . . .

— Why do you suppose it is that the solutions (in some senses) to Nicholas's quest and queries are provided for him by the *mother* of Lily and Rose?

RESEARCH . . .

— Find out about the Greek legend of Demeter. Who was she? In what ways does Lily's mother represent a version of this character? How does the story of Demeter relate to the novel as a whole?

131

Focus on: mystery and the occult

DISTINGUISH AND CONSIDER . . .

— Although there is a lot of the occult in *The Magus*, Fowles presents it as parody. The occult is distinct from a sense of mystery, however: 'A mystery lies at the base of all that is in nature,' he has said, and 'mystery really lies in things the author doesn't say and in the gaps in the story. I regard all that [mystery] in books as symbolic of the general mystery in cosmic, existential terms.' Consider the significance of mystery in *The Magus*.

Focus on: the fables and pastiches

BROADEN YOUR UNDERSTANDING . . .

— What is a 'fable'? Look the term up in a glossary of literary terms. Can *The Magus* be accurately described as a fable? What is meant by 'pastiche'? Compare Fowles's pastiche of Victorian literature with the numerous pastiches of Victorian literature in A. S. Byatt's novel *Possession* (1990).

Focus on: film adaptation

COMPARE MEDIA . . .

— In 1968, Guy Green directed an adaptation (from a screenplay originally by Fowles) of *The Magus*, starring Michael Caine, Anthony Quinn and Candice Bergen. Woody Allen once said that if he had to live his life again, he would do it all the same way, except that next time he wouldn't see the film of *The Magus*. (*The Magus* is said to be one of Allen's favourite novels.) To Fowles this adaptation was 'a disaster all the way down the line'. If you're interested in judging the film adaptation of *The*

Magus for yourself, copies are available through the website
http://www.fowlesbooks.com/movie.html
— Fowles has said that 'I do find something distressingly
amoral in the very nature of film and TV – possibly because
the photographed image denies the spectator of virtually all
use of his own imaginative powers. Whereas reading requires
a constant use of the reader's imagination.'

VINTAGE
LIVING
TEXTS

The French Lieutenant's Woman

IN CLOSE-UP

Reading guides for

THE FRENCH LIEUTENANT'S WOMAN

BEFORE YOU BEGIN TO READ . . .

— Read the interview with Fowles. You will see there that he identifies a number of themes and techniques:

- Freedom
- The nineteenth-century novel
- Moral responsibility
- Authorial voice
- Period

Other themes and techniques that may be useful to consider while reading the novel include:

- The creation of atmosphere
- A sense of place
- Men and women
- Love
- The feminine principle

Reading activities: detailed analysis

Focus on: the epigraphs

READ AND INTERPRET . . .

— You will notice that each chapter in this novel is headed
with one, or two, quotations that function as an epigraph to
the chapter. Look over all the epigraphs and consider how
they highlight the novel's double concern of writing within,
and also reflecting upon, the social and literary conventions
of the nineteenth century.

CHAPTER I
(pp. 9–11)

Focus on: setting

NOTE . . .

— Look over this chapter and the description of the bay at
Lyme Regis. How many words in that description are words
that are associated with the body? What is the effect of this
in terms of the way that you might think about the character
of the setting?

Focus on: the date

RESEARCH . . .

— This novel is set very specifically in 1867. Fowles has said that he likes to use *Punch* in order to get a perspective on a particular historical time. Do some research about the historical context. What books were published in that year? Who was on the throne? What were the major political events of the day? What kind of fashions did women wear? (See the Contexts section on p. 193.)

Focus on: time

LOOK OVER . . .

— Read over the chapter and consider how many words and phrases and images relate to the passage of time. Write them down. Your list will include:

● Ancient
● Seven hundred years
● The Armada
● Primitive
● Middle Ages

When you have composed your list ask yourself what time span is dealt with here. How does this sense of a long time perspective affect your idea of the narrative and the persona of the narrator?

Focus on: the telescopist

THINK ABOUT AND REMEMBER . . .

— On p. 11, the narrative introduces the idea of a 'telescopist' watching the scene. What does this suggest about the persona of the narrator? And in what ways may you – the reader – be a voyeur, watching this scene through the 'telescope' of the novel itself?

CHAPTER 2
(pp. 12–16)

Focus on: dialogue

UNDERLINE AND ASSESS . . .

— Underline or jot down all the unusual words that you notice in this chapter. How is the sense of this being a strange and distant world created by using such vocabulary?

RESEARCH . . .

— Fowles has said that the way in which people spoke in the 1860s was more modern than we might expect, and he had to archaise the dialogue to make it sound authentic. Compare his use of dialogue with that in a novel from the 1860s, such as George Eliot's *The Mill on the Floss* (1860) or R. D. Blackmore's *Lorna Doone* (1869). What similarities and differences does the comparison throw into relief? In what ways is dialogue in a novel likely to differ from real dialogue?

COMPARE . . .

— If you have read Fowles's *The Magus*, you will recall that on pp. 167–170 the protagonist meets a girl who is – or is pretending to be – a visitation from the past and said to have been alive at the time of the First World War. Consider how the narrative plays with this idea of the 'estrangement' of dialogue in that episode, and compare the technique with Fowles's use of dialogue in Chapter 2.

141

Focus on: the figure

COMPARE . . .

— This is Fowles's own account of the beginnings of *The French Lieutenant's Woman* in his imagination. How does this opening scene compare with his initial idea?

It started as a visual image. A woman stands at the end of a deserted quay and stares out to sea. That was all. This image rose in my mind one morning when I was still in bed half asleep. It corresponded to no actual incident in my life (or in art) that I can recall, though I have for many years collected obscure books and forgotten prints, all sorts of flotsam and jetsam from the last two or three centuries, relics of past lives – and I suppose this leaves me with a sort of dense hinterland from which such images percolate down to the coast of consciousness.

These mythopoeic 'stills' (they seem almost always static) float into my mind very often. I ignore them, since that is the best way of finding out whether they really are the door into a new world.

So I ignored this image; but it recurred. Imperceptibly it stopped coming to me. I began deliberately to recall it and to try to analyse and hypothesize why it held some sort of imminent power. It was obviously mysterious . . . I began to fall in love with her. Or with her stance. I didn't know which.

CHAPTER 3
(pp. 17–23)

Focus on: Charles

THINK ABOUT CHARACTERISATION . . .
— Look over the chapter and then write down six key words that describe Charles, choosing words from the text. Then close the book and write four or five sentences that describe Charles's character and use all the words that you have written down. Look back at this later on, when you have read to the end of the novel, to see how accurate your ideas were.

CHAPTER 4
(pp. 24–30)

Focus on: the epigraphs

READ AND REFLECT . . .
— Look at the epigraphs to this chapter. Read the chapter and then consider how the quotations relate to what goes on here. In particular, consider the ways in which the sanitation report from *Human Documents of the Victorian Golden Age* may cast light on the situation at Mrs Poulteney's.

CHAPTER 5
(pp. 31–5)

Focus on: Ernestina

THINK ABOUT CHARACTERISATION . . .
— Write down five key words from the text that describe Ernestina. Then compose four or five sentences about her

using those words. Keep this for later and see how your image of her fits with the events that ensue as you read the book.

Focus on: the time scale of the narrative

LOOK AT AND CONSIDER . . .
— On p. 33, we are told that Ernestina, born in 1846, will die on the day that Hitler invaded Poland. How old would she have been then? Why is this piece of information important? We seem to be reading a nineteenth-century novel, but are we?

Focus on: women in the nineteenth century

CONSIDER . . .
— Ernestina decides that she must not think about sex. Read the following extracts from an article published in 1851. How does this help you to place Ernestina and her ways of thinking?

Anon., 'Woman in her Psychological Relations', from the *Journal of Psychological Medicine and Mental Pathology* (London, 1851)

The relations of woman are twofold: material and spiritual — corporeal and moral. By her corporeal nature she is the type and model of BEAUTY; by her spiritual, of GRACE; by her moral, of LOVE. A perfect woman is indeed the most exalted of terrestrial creatures — physically, mentally, morally. The most profound philosophy, and the most universal instincts of the popular mind concur in this doctrine, each in their own way. The sage, the poet, the painter, see in woman the type of excellence; the mirror of the divinest attributes of the Deity; the model of the good and beautiful . . .

. . . It is in that portion of the body in immediate connexion with those parts peculiar to her
organization, that the greatest beauty of form is
found in woman, as though they were the *fons et origo*
[source and origin] of corporeal as well as mental
loveliness. 'The width of the pelvis in woman causes
the obliquity of the thigh bones; the thigh therefore
slopes much more inwards in woman than in man . . .
This inclination of the thigh on the pelvis, and of
the leg on the thigh, which would constitute an
imperfection in man, and a subject of mockery, gives
to woman a peculiar charm . . .' [a quotation from a
nineteenth-century book on anatomy]

. . . It may be questioned, however, whether the
glorious development of the Divine Idea in the
encasing of the procreative organs and centre of
procreative activity be not equalled by the bust on
which the organs for nutrition of the tender offspring are developed. It is to her bosom that woman
instinctively clasps all that she rightly loves – her
bosom, remarkable for the unsurpassable beauty of
its voluptuous contours and graceful inflexions, the
white transparent surface of which is set off with an
azure network, or tinged with the warm glow of
emotions and passions that make it heave in graceful
undulations. The pelvis is the manifestation of the
instinct – the bust expresses the sentiment of love,
within the recesses of the one the embryo man is
conceived and nourished; upon the other, whether
babe or adult, he is hushed to slumber or soothed in
suffering . . .

. . . The comparison which has been instituted
by poets, between the accession of the age of
puberty and the flowering of plants, is as

philosophical as it is graceful. The *blooming* maiden, glorious in the *lumen juventae purpureum*, is well compared to those brilliant flowers, the reproductive organs of which, when fully developed, are surrounded with the most gorgeous tissues – for what reason we know not. Many animals are equally adorned with ornaments, the development of which is contingent on the development of the reproductive organs. Ripe womanhood has a lustre peculiar to itself, but inferior to none . . .

. . . With a wisdom and a foresight most admirable to contemplate, it is so arranged that if by disease, or in any other way, the essential organs of reproduction in the male be rendered imperfect, and be therefore unfit for their office, these attractive appendages are not developed, or if developed already, drop off. It is for this reason that the effeminate man is no favourite with woman. Woman, in virtue of that mysterious chain which binds creation together in one common bond of vitality, is not exempt from this influence of colour and form . . .

. . . The soldier is *par excellence* the most attractive to the sex; his warlike profession, his manly moustache, the scarlet and gold, the nodding plume, the burnished helm of his uniform, his glittering arms, and the tout-ensemble of his accoutrements, often, where there is a special susceptibility to the sexual influence of form and colour, awake strange mysterious emotions in the young female just bursting into womanhood, that quickly shape themselves into a longing desire, the object of which she scarcely comprehends. Different in its origin, but analogous in its nature, is the preference so often given by the more susceptible portion of the sex to the manly sensualist. The vigorous bold front, the ample beard, the broad chest, the firm port, and the eye flashing passion and admiration, too often carry away an amorous female; and she yields to the tempter, against her better judgement, in spite of the earnest entreaties of her friends, and to the utter rupture of the dearest ties – not excluding the maternal. This *enchantment* – which it literally is – this infatuation, is often due to the unrecognised reaction of the physical appearance of the tempter upon the mind of his victim, untrained to self-control, predisposed to the allurement by an excess of reproductive energy, and irresistibly impelled forward to the gratification of the obscure, deep-felt longings he excites by an over-stimulated nervous system . . .

. . . When the young female suffers from irregular action of the ovaria on the system, the natural astuteness and quickness of perception degenerates into mere artfulness or monomaniacal cunning; and it is to this morbid influence of the ovaria on the organ of the mind, that Dr Laycock attributes the extraordinary instances of monomaniacal cunning in females, on record . . .

. . . When cunning is combined with a morbid excitation of the propensity to destroy, such as is manifested in the females of brutes, the effect is sometimes dreadful, and is seen in the perpetration of secret murders by wholesale poisoning, or in secret incendiarism; and if other natural instincts be perverted, the objects of woman's warmest and most disinterested affections may perish by her hand . . .

. . . Cases are by no means infrequent in which the sufferer from this sad derangement is the most intellectual and most amiable of the family; beloved by all, respected, almost worshipped. Hence, when after numerous struggles to repress them, the propensities excited into such fearful and almost supernatural activity, by the ovarian irritation, burst forth beyond all control, and the pet of the family is seen to be the opposite, morally, in every respect to what she had been – irreligious, selfish, slanderous, false, malicious, devoid of affection, thievish in a thousand petty ways, bold – may be erotic, self-willed and quarrelsome – the shock to the family circle and friends is intense; and if the case be not rightly understood, great, and often irreparable, damage is done to correct what seems to be vice, but is really *moral insanity*. Dr Laycock, we are happy to learn, has been able to treat cases of this kind with perfect success, by a course of galvanism directed through the ovaria, and by suitable medication and moral and hygienic treatment.

Perhaps in the whole range of psychology there is no subject so deeply interesting as this; for it is in moral insanity that man's spiritual and moral nature is the most awfully and most distressingly subjected to his corporeal frame. It is a disease undoubtedly much more frequent in the sex [ie. women] than in man; and if the warning voice we shall here raise against all those methods of education, and mental and physical training – all those conventional customs and social habits – all those *fashions* in dress and social intercourse, which stimulate the nervous system generally of the sex, and the sexual system in particular – be at all successful in placing woman in greater safety from this sad clouding of her intellect – this lamentable spoliation of her greatest charms, we shall feel that we have done good services to society and the state . . .

. . . Hence it is very fairly inferred, that a too early development of the sexual functions leads to disease – especially of the nervous system – or, if not to any well-defined form of affection, at least to that state of the nervous system termed 'nervousness', the 'hysterical temperament', 'great sensitiveness' &c., and the leading characteristic of which is an exalted susceptibility of all impressions, or, as Dr Laycock terms it, *affectibility*, and a refinement of the feelings and intellect, such, that the individual is hardly equal to the wear and tear of life . . .

. . . The Creator has provided that all the most attractive traits in woman's person shall indicate either *moral* or *physical fitness* for her duties as woman. The brilliant lips, the transparent clear complexion, indicate health; the whole body, when it is in its fully developed form and functions, indicates perfect capacity and fitness to reproduce the species – to produce not only offspring, but a healthy race; and, with the *physical capacity*, the requisite *moral feelings* and *sentiments*.

CHAPTER 6
(pp. 36–42)

Focus on: vocabulary

EXAMINE THE WORD CHOICE . . .
— Underline or jot down all the elaborate or unusual words in this chapter. If you do not know them, look them up. What is the effect of this word choice here? How does it inform your attitude to Mrs Poulteney?

CHAPTER 7
(pp. 43–8)

Focus on: the idea of the moment

DISCRIMINATE . . .

— Charles experiences a number of sensations that come together to give him an intense appreciation of the moment in a 'kind of Proustian richness of evocation'. The allusion is to a passage in Marcel Proust's *A la recherche du temps perdu* (1913–27) where memories are vividly evoked by the scent of a particular kind of cake being dipped into a tisane. How does the narrative create the sense of this moment here? Try to work out exactly which features help you to focus and recognise the character of Charles's reaction.

Focus on: Sam

RESEARCH AND COMPARE . . .

— The storyteller explains that Sam, the valet in Charles's life, must remind us of Sam Weller in Charles Dickens's *The Pickwick Papers* (1836–7). Read all or some of that book – Chapter XVI may be a good place to start – and compare the character of Sam Weller with that of Sam Farrow.

CHAPTER 8
(pp. 49–55)

Focus on: Darwin

RESEARCH . . .

— You may have noticed that Darwin has already been quoted in an epigraph to an earlier chapter. Consider how his ideas are cited here. You might like to look at some of his works.

There is a useful edition published by Norton and edited by Philip Appleman. It includes annotations and documents which relate to other theories of evolution in the nineteenth century. You might also like to look at a well-known and important critical book by Gillian Beer called *Darwin's Plots: Evolutionary Narrative in Darwin, George Eliot and Nineteenth Century Fiction* (1982). This argues that Darwin employed many fictional methods in relaying his theories, just as many writers of fiction in the nineteenth century – among them George Eliot and Thomas Hardy – made use of Darwin's theories in their novels.

CHAPTER 9
(pp. 56–69)

Focus on: Sarah

DECIPHER . . .

— In some ways Sarah is the most mysterious of the three main characters presented to us so far. Look over this chapter and try to work out the mainsprings of her character. Think back over all that you have already learned about her. How does that information work with this new information? What would you say are her chief characteristics?

Focus on: walking

CONSIDER . . .

— Sarah likes to be able to go out and walk by herself. What does that suggest about her character – especially in terms of the date and setting of the novel?

— Then think about some of these phrases and terms:

- Streetwalker
- To walk the streets
- To walk in the paths of righteousness
- To walk out together
- To walk forward
- To walk tall

— What do they each mean? Walking seems like a natural and harmless enough activity, but in what ways has it been socially and culturally defined? With what kinds of inclinations – good and bad – is it associated?

CHAPTER 10
(pp. 70–5)

Focus on: the garden

CONSIDER THE REFERENCES AND MEANING . . .
— This chapter begins with a description of the landscape of the Undercliff as Charles sets out on a geological expedition. How many words in this description refer to primitive or ancient or unchanging or remote elements in the surrounding world? What sense of the expanse of time does that suggest? How might that long view make the precise constraints of the social mores of 1867 seem absurd? (Remember that we have just seen one such example in Mrs Poulteney's reaction to the information that Sarah walks on Ware Commons.) Note also the lush description of the trees and the plants on the Undercliff. By the time you get to p. 71, this landscape is being described as an 'English Garden of Eden'. Consider the implications of this reference. Over the page some artists and writers who have portrayed gardens are mentioned. How does this add to the idea of the timelessness of nature untamed?

Focus on: the woman asleep

RESEARCH AND COMPARE . . .

— Charles comes across Sarah asleep. Think about the implications of this. She is unconscious and vulnerable; he is aware,
conscious and in control, but strangely moved. Why might this
be?

— Refer to Chapter Nineteen of George Eliot's *Middlemarch*
(1871–2). Will Ladislaw's artist friend Naumann brings him to
look at Dorothea as she stands in the statue gallery of the
Vatican. Dorothea is not asleep, but she is absorbed in her
thoughts. And she is standing by a famous ancient statue, now
known as the 'Sleeping Ariadne', but for some time known as
'Cleopatra'. How do the two scenes compare? Remember that
in both cases this is the beginning of a serious emotional reation
on the part of the man which will lead on to the love affair
to come.

— You might also look up the story of Ariadne in a book of
Greek legends. When you have done so, think about some of
these terms from the story and how they may connect to
Charles and Sarah and their story.

- Abandonment (in both senses)
- The garden island
- The maze
- The thread that is a clue to escape
- Bacchus's rescue

Focus on: paths

DECIDE AND REMEMBER . . .

— On p. 75, the narrative tells us that in this moment 'the
whole Victorian Age was lost. And I do not mean he had taken
the wrong path.' Remember this 'losing' of the age. What does
it suggest? Think about paths and choices and what they mean.

Look up 'path' in a dictionary of quotations. Or read Robert Frost's poem 'The Road Not Taken'. Remember the image of the path – and the choice of path – as you read on.

CHAPTER 11
(pp. 76–86)

Focus on: the narrator

IDENTIFY . . .

— Consider the persona of the narrator. As you look over this chapter, you will see that there are several places where the narrative departs from the strict conventions of setting a novel in the past. Consider the ways in which this is done and find examples. These may include: using colloquial language from the present day ('planet he had just landed on' p. 86); referring to events and circumstances in the present day; giving an opinion. In many ways you need to treat the narrator as a created character in fiction, much as you think of the created characters of Charles, Tina or Sarah. So write down five words that are the keys to that narrator-character, and then write four or five sentences describing him – are you sure it's a him? – using those five words.

CHAPTER 12
(pp. 87–96)

Focus on: the figure

CONSIDER . . .

— '. . . once again that face had an extraordinary effect on him. It was as if after each sight of it, he could not believe its effect, and had to see it again. It seemed to both envelop and reject him; as if she was a figure in a dream, both standing still and yet always receding' (p. 89). How is the image of Sarah built up in this chapter? What is the effect of her mysteriousness, a) on Charles, b) on Mrs Poulteney, c) on you, and d) on the narrator?

Focus on: paths

LOOK BACK . . .
— Look back at the exercise on paths for Chapter 10. Look over this chapter and think about the implications of this image again. In what ways might it be being employed differently here?

CHAPTER 13
(pp. 97–100)

Focus on: the narrator

ASK YOURSELF . . .
— The story stops for a short time while the narrator addresses us directly. How do you feel about this? In some ways this is an argument defending the novel. It shows that this is a storyteller who is up to date with theories of storytelling. But how does this also contribute to the 'character' or persona of the narrator?

RESEARCH AND COMPARE . . .
— Read Chapter Seventeen of George Eliot's *Adam Bede* (1859) entitled 'In Which the Story Pauses a Little'. Or else read Chapter Five of Jane Austen's *Northanger Abbey* (1818). Both of these are examples of passages in 'classic realist' novels where

the action stops to allow the omniscient narrator to explain why novels are important and what they can do. Compare either or both of these chapters with Fowles's version.

Focus on: the fall

THINK OVER AND ASSESS . . .

— Consider the implications of the idea of 'the fall'. What does it mean to 'be fallen'? What is a 'fallen woman'? What does it mean to 'fall from grace'? What is 'the fall of man'? On pp. 99–100, several jumpings or fallings are mentioned. In the largest sense, what is it that is being discussed or suggested here?

CHAPTER 14
(pp. 101–7)

Focus on: social convention and expectation

ASSESS . . .

— On p. 106 Charles and Sarah look at each other and acknowledge a 'common enemy'. How does this moment overturn convention? What does this suggest about their actual and possible relationship to each other?

CHAPTER 15
(pp. 108–11)

Focus on: men and women and class

COMPARE . . .

— The first section of this chapter deals with Charles and Ernestina's relationship. The second, with an account of Sam and Mary's relationship. In what ways are these two scenes different? In what ways are they similar?

CHAPTER 16
(pp. 112–24)

Focus on: Sarah

CONTRAST AND COMPARE . . .
— Compare Ernestina with Sarah, and compare Charles's relationships with each of the two women. How is Sarah's 'mystery' being unfolded?

NOTE AND REMEMBER . . .
— Charles expresses some anxiety that Sarah will fall and turn her ankle while out alone on the Undercliff (p. 118). Remember this episode. It will become important later on.

CHAPTER 17
(pp. 125–33)

Focus on: vocabulary

LOOK OVER . . .
— This chapter uses words and phrases specific to 1867 and specific to the late twentieth century. Underline as many conflicting examples as you can. Then ask yourself how this double perspective – as conveyed in this language – contributes to the tone of the novel, and to your attitudes as you read.

CHAPTER 18
(pp. 134–44)

Focus on: allusions

LOOK UP . . .
— On p. 140, there is a reference to a siren, and to Odysseus and Calypso. If you do not know the origins of these stories, look them up and then consider how they might relate to the events shown here.

ASK YOURSELF . . .
— What is happening to Charles?

LINK AND INTERPRET . . .
— 'He knew he was about to engage in the forbidden, or rather the forbidden was about to engage in him' (p. 144). In what ways does this relate to a) the image of the garden and of Eden that was set up in Chapter 10, and b) the image of paths and a choosing of paths? Look also at the end of the chapter where we are told that Charles is like a man who had 'stepped off the Cobb and set sail for China' (p. 144).

CHAPTER 19
(pp. 145–59)

Focus on: women, melancholia and sexuality

COMPARE AND CONTRAST . . .
— Dr Grogan diagnoses Sarah's problem as melancholia (p. 151). From the 1840s on, there was much medical and scientific interest in physical and mental problems manifested by women. Some nineteenth-century ideas on this topic may

seem laughable now, but many young women suffered as a result of diagnoses of this kind and the unfortunate treatments that were prescribed. If you are interested in this subject, you may like to read some recent critical and theoretical books on the subject, such as Elaine Showalter's *The Female Malady: Women, Madness and English Culture 1830–1980* (1987), Janet Bezier's *Ventriloquized Bodies: Narratives of Hysteria in Nineteenth Century France* (1994), or Elisabeth Bronfen, *The Knotted Subject: Hysteria and Its Discontents* (1998).

ASSESS . . .
— On pp. 154–6, the narrative sets up a picture of Sarah and Millie in bed and then explains that this was 1867 so we needn't worry. In what ways does this passage help to explain the difference between 'then' and 'now' in terms of our assumptions about sexuality and social propriety? And in what ways might this reference highlight modern obsessions and fears?

Focus on: Darwin

RESEARCH THE CONTEXT. . .
— Charles and Dr Grogan discuss Darwin and his theories of evolution. Quite a bit of information is given to you here on this subject, but if you need more then it would be a good idea to read some of Darwin's *The Origin of Species* (1859).
— Look up these terms and jot down a definition of each:

- Adaptation
- Evolution
- 'The survival of the fittest'
- The biblical Creation story
- Modification
- Natural selection

CHAPTER 20
(pp. 160–73)

Focus on: reference

NOTE AND CONSIDER . . .

— The second epigraph to this chapter is a quotation concerning a scene that took place after the assassination of the American President John F. Kennedy in Dallas in 1963. His wife had been with him in the open-topped car. When the fatal bullets were fired she crawled backwards out of the car, but not before she had been splattered with the blood and brains of her husband. When Lyndon B. Johnson, the Vice-President, arrived in Dallas later that day to be sworn in as serving President, Jacqueline Kennedy insisted on being present, but refused to change out of her pink linen – and stained – dress. Think about this story when you have read to the end of the chapter, and consider how it relates to and illuminates the story that Sarah tells.

Focus on: the image of the chosen path and the image of the fall

LIST AND ASSESS . . .

— In the course of the scene between Sarah and Charles, several references are made to the idea of the 'path' and the idea of the 'fall'. Note down as many such allusions as you can. How do these help to emphasise the metaphors in terms of the unfolding plot?

Looking over Chapters 1–20

QUESTIONS FOR DISCUSSION OR ESSAYS

1. 'Lyme Regis and its surrounding countryside is as much a character as a setting.' Do you agree?

2. How does Fowles deal with the theme of freedom in the novel so far?

3. 'The narrator is the most important character in the book.' Discuss.

4. Compare the methods and narrative techniques used by Fowles in *The French Lieutenant's Woman* with the methods and narrative techniques used in any ONE nineteenth-century novel.

5. Consider the image and idea of 'the fossil' in the novel so far.

6. Assess the function of the chapter epigraphs in the novel.

CHAPTER 21
(pp. 174–82)

Focus on: identity and self-definition

ANALYSE . . .
— In what ways is Sarah's taking on herself the role of 'outcast' also the means of providing her with an identity?

Focus on: the moment

LOOK FOR A PATTERN . . .
— Charles has another one of those intense experiences when he understands the significance of the moment. How much of the plotting of the novel so far has been built up around just such specific moments? How does the portrayal of those moments connect to the novel's themes of freedom, choice and moral responsibility?

161

CHAPTER 22
(pp. 183–8)

Focus on: irony and rhetoric

IDENTIFY THE EFFECTS . . .

— The narrator – or narrative persona – shows himself (itself) to be aware of the rhetorical and formal procedures being used here. On p. 184 we read, 'I am mixing metaphors – but that was how Charles's mind worked.' Where else in this chapter is there evidence of irony and the use of rhetoric? Look particularly for repetitions, italics and parentheses. How does the fact that attention is being drawn to these techniques by the narrative itself affect your attitude to the characters or to the 'realism' of the novel?

CHAPTER 23
(pp. 189–93)

Focus on: Charles's expectations

READ AND COMPARE . . .

— Charles returns home to Winsyatt in the sure knowledge that the estate will be his and in the expectation that his uncle will invite him to choose which property he will live in with his new bride. In fact, things will turn out very differently.

— Read Chapter 44 of George Eliot's *Adam Bede* where Arthur Donnisthorne returns to his family estate after the death of his grandfather, certain that he will now inherit all this and making happy plans for the future. What he does not know – though we know – is that Hetty Sorrel, a villager whom he had seduced the previous summer, has been arrested and is on trial accused of murdering her baby. Compare these two chapters setting out expectations defeated and overturned.

Focus on: Sarah

ASK YOURSELF . . .
— At the end of this chapter we see Sarah choosing to walk
— and to be seen walking — across Ware Commons. Why do
you think she does what she does?

CHAPTER 24
(pp. 194–8)

Focus on: Ernestina and Sarah

CONTRAST . . .
— In what ways might you make a comparison between
Ernestina's behaviour, as described in this chapter, and Sarah's?
What contrast is being set up between the two women?

CHAPTER 25
(pp. 199–203)

Focus on: time and the ammonite

NOTE AND REMEMBER . . .
— On p. 200 Charles perceives time as a horizontal axis, as
opposed to a vertical one. Keep this image in mind as you
read. You will find that it comes back again and becomes a
significant marker in Charles's personal history.

COMPARE . . .
— Look up Chapter 22 of Thomas Hardy's novel *A Pair of
Blue Eyes* (1873). The hero has accidentally fallen over the edge
of a cliff but manages to obtain a foothold and clings on while

he waits for assistance. Here he find himself staring at a fossil in the cliff face and is thus brought to consider time, its passage and the implications for individual existence. How does this comparison help to situate Charles's own image of the trilobite?

Focus on: the narrator

EVALUATE . . .

— 'I am overdoing the exclamation marks,' says the narrator (p. 202). Evaluate the importance of this intervention. What does it suggest about the way that the narrative persona constitutes the fictional character of Charles? What does it suggest about the relation between the narrator – or the narrating persona – and the reader? To help you assess this, consider this list of terms. Which is most appropriate?

- Intimate
- Critical
- Dismissive
- Dictatorial
- Knowing
- Authoritative

CHAPTER 26
(pp. 204–12)

Focus on: analeptic

CONSIDER THE EFFECT . . .

— This chapter takes us back to the events that took place earlier in the day at Winsyatt, firstly in explaining to us what happened in the servants' hall, and then in giving us a picture of the scene enacted between Charles and his uncle. Why do you suppose we are given this flashback at this point? How does it affect the pace of the unfolding events? And how does it manipulate your attitude to those unfolding events?

CHAPTER 27
(pp. 213–22)

Focus on: Dr Grogan

THINK ABOUT DOCTORS AND PRIESTS . . .

— There is no priest in this novel (other than the vicar we met in Chapter 40) but there is a doctor. On p. 214, you will see that there is a generalising paragraph about the role of priests and doctors and their capacity to discern and understand deceit. Think about doctors (or priests) in literature. There is Lydgate in George Eliot's *Middlemarch*, Ezra Jennings in Wilkie Collins's *The Moonstone* (1868), Dr Watson in Conan Doyle's Sherlock Holmes stories (1887 on). How might any of these earlier portraits of literary doctors be compared with Fowles's Dr Grogan?

CHAPTER 28
(pp. 223–31)

Focus on: hysteria

RESEARCH AND COMPARE . . .

— During the course of the nineteenth century, many doctors and scientists began to study the functioning of the female body, and in particular the character and progress of certain kinds of diseases that were considered to be psychosexual in origin. Read these extracts from two works published in 1848 and 1853 respectively. How might the terms of these extracts compare with the examples cited in this chapter?

Dr J. C. Millingen
The Passions; or, Mind and Matter,
London, 1848

If corporeal agency is thus powerful in man, its tyrannic influence will more frequently cause the misery of the gentler sex. Woman, with her exalted spiritualism, is more forcibly under the control of matter; her sensations are more vivid and acute, her sympathies more irresistible. She is less under the influence of the brain than the uterine system, the plexi of abdominal nerves, and irritation of the spinal cord; in her, hysteric predisposition is incessantly predominating from the dawn of puberty. Therefore is she subject to all the aberrations of love and religion; ecstatic under the impression of both, the latter becomes a resource when the excitement of the former is exhausted by disappointment, infidelity, and age . . .

. . . But alas! If women are frail, and may occasionally deserve the harsh epithets bestowed upon them, to what are we to attribute their sad destiny? Simply *to their organisation, their education, and our injustice.* What is dishonour in them, is the boast and pride of man; and their fall constitutes his triumph . . .

. . . I cannot better conclude these observations, than by quoting a passage of one of our most able and philosophic physiologists, who thus expresses himself on the subject: 'There is no obvious structural difference in the nervous system of the two sexes, save the inferior size of the cerebral hemisphere in the female. This difference, which is not observed in other parts of the encephalon, is readily accounted for, when we compare the psychical character of woman with that of man. For there can be no doubt that, putting aside the exceptional cases, which then occur, the intellectual powers of woman are inferior to those of men. Although her perceptive faculties are more acute, her capability of sustaining mental exertion is much less; and though her views are often peculiarly distinguished by clearness and decision, they are in general deficient in that comprehensiveness which is necessary for their stability. With less of the *volitional* power that man possesses, she has the *emotional* and *instinctive* in a much stronger degree. The emotions therefore predominate, and more frequently become the leading springs of action than they are in man.

. . . In regard to the inferior development of her intellectual powers, therefore, and in the predominance of the instinctive, woman must be considered as ranking below man; but in the superior purity and elevation of her feelings she is as highly raised above him. Her whole character, physical as well as corporeal, is beautifully adapted to supply what is deficient in man, and to elevate and refine those powers which might otherwise be directed to low and selfish objects.

R. B. Carter
On the Pathology and Treatment of Hysteria,
London, 1853

If the relative power of emotion against the sexes be compared in the present day, even without

THE FRENCH LIEUTENANT'S WOMAN

including the erotic passion, it is seen to be considerably greater in the woman than in the man, partly from that natural conformation which causes the former to feel, under circumstances where the latter thinks; and partly because the woman is more often under the necessity of endeavouring to conceal her feelings. But when sexual desire is taken into the account, it will add immensely to the forces bearing upon the female, who is often much under its dominion; and who, if unmarried and chaste, is compelled to restrain every manifestation of its sway. Man, on the contrary, has such facilities for its gratification, that as a source of disease it is almost inert against him, and when powerfully excited, it is pretty sure to be speedily exhausted through the proper channel.

. . . The greatest difficulty which has hitherto presented itself to writers on the disease under consideration, has depended upon its distinct association, in the majority of cases, with the sexual propensities of the female, and with derangements of her sexual organs, while, at the same time, it cannot be connected with any one kind of derangement rather than with others, or with desire rather than with loathing, except in the usual numerical proportion which exists between the different states. Hence many endeavours have been made to discover a common action exerted by them all, and (without regard to the cases in which none of them are apparent) the phenomena have been accounted for by the employment of a word which is useful to express ignorance rather than knowledge; that is, they have been referred to *irritation* of the uterus and ovaria . . .

. . . The female reproductive organs having a cause peculiar to themselves to make them the subjects of attention, and being equally exposed with all the rest of the body to the influence of sensations and of suggestions from without – suffer from determination of blood more frequently and more severely than other parts. The power of the last mentioned cause has been greatly extended and increased by the researches of gentlemen engaged in the treatment of uterine disease, and by the consequent discovery that a very large number of our countrywomen are invalided by some of its numerous forms. It is scarcely possible at present for an hysterical girl to have no acquaintances among the many women who are subjected to the speculum and caustic, and who love to discuss their symptoms and to narrate the sensations which attend upon their treatment . . .

. . . In many cases ladies are quite ignorant of the nature of the remedies administered to them; and even if they heard the name of Indian hemp, would scarcely know the purposes for which it has long been used by the Hindoos; but still they may possibly find out by observation that the speculum becomes grateful to their feelings the oftener it is applied, and that the wish for it is in some degree excited by each successive dose of the medicine; an induction which, when arrived at, they are very likely to communicate to their friends. So much has been written on this subject by abler men, that some apology is demanded for alluding to it here; but this may be furnished by the plea that the indiscriminate employment of the speculum is both a disgrace to the medical profession, and a misfortune to the female sex, in a nation where chastity and modesty have been esteemed and practised amongst us. Not long since I travelled in a railway carriage with a stranger, who presently entered into conversation, and said (without knowing the profession of his fellow-passengers) that he had applied caustic to the wombs of twelve women on that morning, making the statement with an air of great exultation, and proceeding to describe himself as a country general practitioner, and a resident of South Wales . . .

RESEARCH AND COMPARE . . .

— Just as issues to do with female sexuality were widely written about and discussed in scientific and medical circles in the nineteenth century, so this contemporary concern found its way into the literature of the period. Important novels that include some discussion of delusion, hysteria (not necessarily so named), madness and psychosexual disorder might include Charlotte Brontë's *Jane Eyre* (1847), Wilkie Collins's *The Woman in White* (1860), Mary Braddon's *Lady Audley's Secret* (1862), or Charlotte Perkins Gilman *The Yellow Wallpaper* (1892). Read any one – or more – of these novels and consider the ways in which their themes and concerns connect to this 'pastiche' nineteenth-century novel in *The French Lieutenant's Woman*.

Focus on: the theme of freedom

LINK . . .

— On p. 229 the narrative tells us, 'He had never felt less free.' Why does Charles feel like this? Why is it important to the themes of the novel? Look back at the interview with Fowles (pp. 14–17) and consider the ways in which he discusses the issue of 'freedom' there.

Focus on: the ammonite

REMEMBER AND ASK . . .

— Remember Charles's relationship to the ammonite and his wish to break away from 'vertical' time. Look over your notes if you made some. If not, look back for Charles's thoughts on fossils and ask yourself: what might make Charles feel free, and what is making him feel 'not free'?

CHAPTER 29
(pp. 232–5)

Focus on: the garden

LOOK BACK . . .

— Charles goes up to the Undercliff. Look at the description of the landscape and the morning. What does it remind you of? When have we been here before – both in terms of scene and in terms of metaphor? What does this suggest about what is about to happen?

Focus on: plotting

ANALYSE . . .

— Why does this chapter end as Charles looks over the partition? As a reader, how are you being manipulated? Do you mind? What is the effect of this 'cliffhanger'? With what types of literature – or drama – are such devices most usually associated?

CHAPTER 30
(pp. 236–8)

Focus on: analeptic

ANALYSE THE NARRATIVE STRATEGY . . .
— Why do you suppose that we are given this flashback to
the scene that occurred between Sarah and Mrs Poulteney just
at this point in the narrative? ·

CHAPTER 31
(pp. 239–43)

Focus on: the centre

RELATE . . .
— If you look towards the end of the book, you will see that
there are sixty-one chapters in all, which means that the
episodes recounted here are more or less at the centre of the
book. Can you make an argument to propose that that is how
it should be? That the events recounted here are central to the
themes and concerns of the novel as a whole?

Focus on: the sleeping woman

COMPARE AND INFER . . .
— This is not the first time that we have seen Sarah asleep,
nor the first time that Charles has seen Sarah asleep. Think
over the episodes where Charles saw her in this way. But think
also over the scenes where the narrative has presented her in
bed, asleep, or simply in her private room. What does this suggest about Charles and his relationship to Sarah? What does
this suggest about the narrator – or the narrating persona –
and his relationship to Sarah?

Focus on: plotting

QUESTION . . .
— Another cliffhanger occurs at the end of this chapter
(p. 243). Why?

CHAPTER 32
(pp. 244–7)

Focus on: analeptic

ANALYSE THE EFFECT . . .
— Here is another flashback, this time to Ernestina's thoughts
and situation. Why do you think it happens now? What is the
effect on you? Do you care about her? If not, why not?

CHAPTER 33
(pp. 248–52)

Focus on: worlds

CONNECT . . .
— Sarah represents 'worlds' (p. 252). How does this connect
to the themes of intermeshing worlds as they are played out
in the novel? How many 'worlds' have you already seen? Look
again at the first chapter and the long perspective into ancient
history. Consider the collision of the nineteenth-century novel
and a twentieth-century viewpoint. Think about the class
clashes in this story. Add in the idea of the powerless or unfree
'ammonite' that haunts Charles's imagination.

CHAPTER 34
(pp. 253–7)

Focus on: the narrator

DECODE . . .

— 'Meanwhile, Charles can get up to London on his own' (p. 257). The narrator feigns a lack of interest in the mechanics of the plotting of the novel. Why is this? Where do your own interests lie now as the story progresses?

CHAPTER 35
(pp. 258–64)

Focus on: Victorian sexuality

INVESTIGATE . . .

— Look at the second epigraph. Think carefully about the context and then ask yourself what you think 'insulted' means. Did these boys call this girl rude names – that is what we would understand by the term now – or did they do something more?

— In many ways we have a very anodyne idea of Victorian sexuality, and in this chapter the narrator, from the point of view of 1969, is trying to explain how research into actual documents of the period shows something quite different. Think, for instance, about the phrase 'Victorian values', which in colloquial language of the late twentieth and early twentieth-first century may still include some idea of piety and sexual repression. As the narrator points out here, the facts of nineteenth-century history were otherwise. Useful books on this area include Steven Marcus's *The Other Victorians* (1969), Michael Mason's *The Making of Victorian Sexuality* (1994), and Judith Walkowitz's *The City of Dreadful Night* (1993).

— One way of thinking about this topic would be to find out about the idea of 'the age of consent'. What does it mean? What is the socially constraining concept behind the legislation? When was it first instituted? What age is it set at today? Has it ever been set at any other age, and if so, what was that?

— If may be helpful to look up the name of Josephine Butler on the Internet, or the Contagious Diseases Acts of 1864, 1866 and 1869, and the Labouchere Amendment to the Criminal Law Amendment Act of 1885.

Focus on: allusion

RESEARCH AND COMPARE . . .

— Towards the end of this chapter the narrative mentions Thomas Hardy and his two characters Sue Bridehead and Tess Durbeyfield. If you have read either *Tess of the D'Urbervilles* (1891) or *Jude the Obscure* (1894), then compare the picture of Victorian female sexuality given there to that which is presented in *The French Lieutenant's Woman*.

CHAPTER 36
(pp. 265–70)

Focus on: the bandage

NOTE . . .

— We are told that one of Sarah's purchases is a bandage (p. 269). Remember this. It will become important later on.

CHAPTER 37
(pp. 271–9)

Focus on: fathers and uncles

COMPARE . . .
— Charles goes to see Mr Freeman, Ernestina's father. What kind of a father do you think he is? How does this scene between him and Charles compare with the scene between Charles and his uncle in Chapter 26?

Focus on: the theme of freedom

ANALYSE . . .
— One of the major themes of this novel is the idea of freedom. If you look back at the interview with Fowles, you will see that he discusses it there on pp. 14–17. How ironic is it that Mr Freeman has this name? How free is he?

CHAPTER 38
(pp. 280–7)

Focus on: class distinction

CONSIDER . . .
— Charles thinks about Mr Freeman's proposition. He looks around at London and he considers the strata or layers of society. Remember that this is set in 1867, and consider the presentation of class distinction set out in this chapter.

CHAPTERS 39 AND 40
(pp. 288–304)

Focus on: Victorian sexuality

COMPARE AND CONTRAST . . .
— Charles visits a brothel with his friends, then picks up a girl. How does the one public performance compare and contrast with the second, private reality?

Looking over Chapters 21–40

QUESTIONS FOR DISCUSSION OR ESSAYS
1. 'The past is a foreign country: they do things differently there' (L. P. Hartley). Discuss, in relation to *The French Lieutenant's Woman*.

2. Examine the theme of freedom in the novel so far.

3. How is the idea of evolution and the Darwinian concept of 'the survival of the fittest' played out in the novel so far?

4. Compare and contrast the different settings of the novel to this point: Lyme Regis, the Undercliff, Winsyatt, London.

5. What is the significance of 'paths' and the choosing of paths?

CHAPTER 41
(pp. 305–9)

Focus on: the child

INTERPRET . . .
— Charles is kind to the child as her mother is kind to him. It is often (but not always) the case that characters' attitudes

to children, animals and servants tell you something about their personality in a novel. What do you make of Charles's behaviour with this child on this occasion?

CHAPTER 42
(pp. 310–18)

Focus on: letters

TRANSFORM . . .

— Look at the two letters and one telegram given in this chapter. Consider the style and method of expression in each. Then take Charles's letter to Dr Grogan on p. 311 and transform it. Rewrite it so that it is 'honest' and tells Grogan the truth about Charles's meeting with Sarah and his current attitude towards her. Is it easy to do this in a language which is appropriate to 1867? How does this help you to analyse what kind of state Charles may be in?

CHAPTER 43
(pp. 319–21)

Focus on: paths and fossils

CONSIDER THE IMAGE . . .

— On p. 320, Charles decides that he cannot face any more 'prevarication' and tells Sam to get a carriage to take them to Lyme. He has made a choice, taken a path. On p. 321, the narrative sets up the analogy with the hapless ammonite and explains that his hopes of freedom are now 'extinct' and that his potential will now become a 'fossil'. Look back over the novel and try to find as many places as you can where this image has been used to develop the processes and stages of Charles's 'evolution'. In what ways might Fowles be setting up the idea that the story of Charles's experiences is, in effect, parallel to a story of Darwinian 'adaptation' that allows for 'survival' through change? Note: if any of these terms are strange to you, look back at the exercise for Chapter 19, or look them up in Philip Appleman's edition of Darwin's *On the Origins of Species* (1979) or Gillian Beer's *Darwin's Plots: Evolutionary Narrative in Darwin, George Eliot and Nineteenth Century Fiction* (1982).

CHAPTER 44
(pp. 322–6)

Focus on: endings

WEIGH UP . . .

— Charles goes back to Ernestina, presents her with the brooch, marries her and they produce seven children, while Mrs Poulteney dies and is refused entry into heaven. We are told that this is the end of the story. But even while you are reading it, you can see that this can hardly be so as there are still some 150 pages to go. What else, in the narrator's tone, may make you distrust his assertion that we are at the end of the story? Look also at the assertion on p. 325 that Charles would survive Ernestina by a decade and mourn her 'earnestly' throughout it. Do you know when Ernestina is supposed to have died? And what's not quite right about the choice of adverb describing his mode of mourning?

CHAPTER 45
(pp. 327–30)

Focus on: choice and freedom

RELATE . . .
— Read what happens, then consider how this chapter relates to the major themes of choice and freedom.

Focus on: Sarah

ANALYSE . . .
— Look at the passage on p. 328 where the narrative tells us how Charles was tormented by Sarah's three-word letter. Look up the meaning of 'Delphic'. How has Sarah set up a mode of brief but meaningful communication with Charles? And what has that done to him and why?

CHAPTER 46
(pp. 331–7)

Focus on: surprise

ASK YOURSELF . . .
— Are you surprised by what happens?

Focus on: time

COMPARE . . .
— Time is mentioned in this chapter. Look back at Chapter 1 and the notes you made about the length of time, the perspective being offered to us by the narrating voice there. How do the two compare and contrast?

Focus on: the bandage

CONNECT . . .

— Where have you seen this bandage before? What is odd about the fact that you have encountered it before?

CHAPTER 47
(pp. 338–43)

Focus on: surprise

ASK YOURSELF . . .

— Are you surprised (again) by what happens? How have your expectations been manipulated?

Focus on: 1867 or 1969?

DISCRIMINATE . . .

— What elements in the language or the attitudes set out in this chapter belong to 1867, and which belong to 1969? How does the double focus affect your response to the story?

CHAPTER 48
(pp. 344–52)

Focus on: choice and freedom

ASSESS . . .

— In what ways are these themes paramount in this chapter?

CHAPTER 49
(pp. 353–9)

Focus on: then and now

ANALYSE . . .
— 'Every Victorian had two minds' (p. 355). In what ways is this one of the major themes of the book? And how is that theme set out in terms of the techniques and narrative methods that Fowles uses?

Focus on: letters

LOOK BACK AND COMPARE . . .
— Consider Charles's letter to Sarah on pp. 355–7. How does it compare with the other letters that he has written in the past? In what ways has his style – and his self-conception and self-presentation – changed?

CHAPTER 50
(pp. 360–9)

Focus on: Darwin

CONNECT . . .
— Read the epigraph to this chapter, a quotation about 'modification' and 'natural selection' from Darwin's *The Origin of Species*. How does this quotation relate to the events that take place in the chapter? And how do these events connect to the overall theme of 'evolution' in the story?

CHAPTER 51
(pp. 370–3)

Focus on: allusion

LOOK UP . . .

— Charles feels like a traitor, like 'a Judas, an Ephialtes' (p. 371). One of these is a familiar name, the other is not. Look up both their stories and consider how they help your understanding of Charles's position.

Focus on: class distinction

DISCRIMINATE . . .

— Charles having said his say with Ernestina, Sam comes to remonstrate with him. Compare the language and the manners exhibited in the two scenes of confrontation in Chapters 50 and 51. What distinctions are made by virtue of gender difference and class difference?

CHAPTER 52
(pp. 374–7)

Focus on: reactions

LIST AND INTERPRET . . .

— Write down three key terms that describe the reactions to the announcement in this chapter, on the part of Aunt Tranter, Mary and Ernestina. Who is most interested in what?

CHAPTER 53
(pp. 378–82)

Focus on: evolution and the theme of freedom

CONSIDER AND ANALYSE . . .
— Read this chapter very carefully. Remember that Dr Grogan is a fellow 'Darwinian'. Remember also that he and Charles have had occasion to discuss Sarah and the conventions of the age that restrict the capacities of women – and men too. Note that Charles clearly tells the absolute truth – in all its details – to Grogan. What is different, therefore, about this scene from the many more conventional ones that have gone before? In what ways does Charles and Grogan's discussion of 'law', 'the world' and 'freedom' contribute to the playing out of the theme in the novel as a whole? Why do you suppose, in the end, that Grogan, as it were, gives Charles his blessing?

CHAPTER 54
(pp. 383–6)

Focus on: expectation

RELATE . . .
— Relate this new experience of reversed expectation and loss to the others that Charles has undergone in the course of the story. In what ways is his reaction to this event different from his earlier reactions? How and in what ways is his character 'evolving'.

CHAPTER 55
(pp. 387–90)

Focus on: the stranger

ASK YOURSELF . . .

— Ask yourself who might this stranger be who is travelling on the train with Charles. What is the significance of his intervention? How does the chapter's epigraph connect to the content of the chapter?

CHAPTER 56
(pp. 391–9)

Focus on: breach of promise

COMPARE AND CONTRAST . . .

— One of the most famous cases in literature of the bringing of a 'breach of promise' action is that which takes place in Dickens's *The Pickwick Papers*. Read Chapter 26, relating to the case brought by Mrs Bardell against Pickwick. Charles's encounter with Mr Freeman is rather more serious and nastier. But in what other ways might these two fictional episodes be compared?

CHAPTER 57
(pp. 400–6)

Focus on: Sam's story

GAUGE . . .

— Sam and Mary's story has a happy conclusion. But we know that Sam has a guilty conscience. While Charles has changed and left behind the 'Victorian' age, in what ways has Sam remained the same and essentially a product of his time?

CHAPTER 58
(pp. 407–12)

Focus on: the mysterious aloof woman

IDENTIFY . . .
— Many of Fowles's fictions are based on the image of the mysterious woman who is always at a distance. This is what Sarah has been – and is still. If you know his novels *The Collector* and *The Magus*, identify different treatments of the same themes there.

CONNECT . . .
— On pp. 410–11, Charles wonders if he has not conjured up the 'Sarah' he dreams of: 'He became increasingly unsure of the frontier between the real Sarah and the Sarah he had created in so many such dreams: the one Eve personified, all mystery and love and profundity, and the other a half-scheming, half-crazed governess from an obscure seaside town.' How does this consideration, this doubt, connect to the themes and literary methods of the novel as a whole?

CHAPTER 59
(pp. 413–18)

Focus on: America

RELATE . . .
— What does it add to Charles's transformation that he should travel to America and find it a different – and a more liber-

ated – society from the one he left behind in England? How does this episode relate to the themes of the novel as a whole?

CHAPTER 60
(pp. 419–39)

Focus on: famous men

FIND OUT . . .

— On p. 423, Charles sees a man he recognises: 'For this was a face he knew; a face he had even once listened to for an hour or more, with Ernestina beside him.' Given that this recognisable man must have been giving a lecture, it seems likely that this person is John Ruskin. Find out about his work. You might even like to read some of his writings. He wrote on art but also on social considerations. His essay 'Of Queen's Gardens' is a well-known statement on his theories on the relations between men and women and their 'separate spheres' of influence.

Focus on: Dante Gabriel Rossetti and the Pre-Raphaelites

RESEARCH . . .

— The so-called 'Pre-Raphaelite' group who were working in the mid to late nineteenth century included such artists, writers and thinkers as Dante Gabriel Rossetti, his sister Christina and brother William Michael, William Morris, Holman Hunt, John Everett Millais, Arthur Hughes, William Bell Scott and Edward Burne-Jones. Though they did not necessarily conceive of themselves and their work as a 'movement', their ideals about accuracy of representation in painting (going back, notionally, to a simple and honest style that was 'pre-Raphael') were highly influential; as were their ideas and those people around them on beauty, ornament, the value of the individual life and the dignity of labour. There were several major retrospectives and exhibitions of their work in the late twentieth century, including one at the Whitechapel Art Gallery and another at the Tate, and their influence is still considerable today. If you would like to know more about them – and how to place Sarah's relation to their philosophies – then you might like to look up the movement on the Internet, or read any of the many books or exhibition catalogues on their life, art and work.

REFLECT . . .
— To Fowles, Rossetti – both as a personality and as a major painter of the nineteenth century – symbolises a breakthrough, standing up against the phoney piousness of the age: 'The Pre-Raphaelite movement was one of the key movements in working out that awful straitjacketed, puritanical aspect of the Victorian age.' In the light of this comment, consider the significance of Rossetti appearing as a mentor for Sarah in *The French Lieutenant's Woman*.

Focus on: Lalage

CONNECT . . .
— Why might 'Lalage' be a good name for Sarah's baby? Charles helpfully gives a translation on p. 438.

Focus on: parables

LOOK BACK . . .
— On p. 439 Charles says to Sarah: 'Shall I ever understand your parables?' Think over your experience of reading the whole novel. What parables have you heard? If you're not sure of the strict meaning of the term, look it up.

CHAPTER 61
(pp. 440–5)

Focus on: the 'extremely important-looking person'

GAUGE THE IRONY . . .

— Who might this person be that appears rather suddenly on the embankment on p. 440? Note that he has a beard. Have you met this character before in the novel? A clue: he was on a railway train. Another clue: look at the inside back cover of your copy of the novel. What ironies are created by Fowles appearing in his own novel?

Focus on: endings

DECIDE FOR YOURSELF . . .

— Here you are given two endings to the story of Charles and Sarah, one in Chapter 60 and this in Chapter 61. Which do you prefer, and why? You might like to look at the interview with Fowles where he says that – for himself – he prefers the 'happy' ending (p. 16). He also explains why, seeing Sarah as the vehicle for Charles's salvation and new freedom. How would you explain that 'freedom' to someone else? Is Charles – as a result of his experiences while separated from Sarah – still, to some degree, 'freer' than he was, whatever the outcome of his relationship with her?

LOOK BACK AT THE BEGINNING AND COMPARE . . .

— Look at the end of Chapter 61 on p. 445. How does this ending – and the allusion to Matthew Arnold's poem – connect back to the beginning of the story?

Looking over the whole novel

QUESTIONS FOR DISCUSSION OR ESSAYS

1. What contemporary relevance does *The French Lieutenant's Woman* have?

2. How does *The French Lieutenant's Woman* develop the theme of the male exploitation of women?

3. Can *The French Lieutenant's Woman* be accurately described as a feminist text?

4. 'How you achieve freedom . . . All my books are about that' (Fowles). How useful is this as a description of what *The French Lieutenant's Woman* is about?

5. '*The French Lieutenant's Woman* advocates the importance of passion and of the imagination.' Discuss.

6. '*The French Lieutenant's Woman* was really an exercise in technique – a complex bit of literary gymnastics.' Is this a fair assessment of the novel, in your opinion?

7. What attitudes to the nineteenth century do you find in *The French Lieutenant's Woman*?

8. Does *The French Lieutenant's Woman* advocate a distinct morality, in your opinion?

9. 'The existential thesis of *The French Lieutenant's Woman* is that one has to discover one's feelings.' Discuss.

10. 'Charles and Sarah are both meant to be determined by

history and challenged with choosing for themselves' (Fowles). Discuss.

11. 'Sarah Woodruff was deliberately created to suggest the "beneficial" side of the historical exile [of women . . .] which allows them to stand outside the ritual games and role-mania of the average male' (Fowles). Discuss Sarah Woodruff's portrayal in the light of this comment.

12. Consider the idea that in *The French Lieutenant's Woman* it is Fowles's female characters who are the repositories of 'right feeling'.

13. What does *The French Lieutenant's Woman* have to say about how much real freedom the individual has in a world shaped by hereditary and environmental forces of an unpredictable kind?

14. Discuss the richness of Fowles's language in *The French Lieutenant's Woman*.

15. 'I do love realism on the surface, but I also love the enormous artifice that writing involves' (Fowles). Discuss *The French Lieutenant's Woman* with reference to this comment.

16. In what ways does Fowles's use of 'metafiction' – of narrative self-consciousness – add complexity to *The French Lieutenant's Woman*?

17. 'Sarah is a distinctively twentieth-century creation.' Discuss.

18. 'Lyme Regis is more a character than a setting.' Do you agree?

19. Consider the proposition that Fowles's novel is a modern version of an 'evolutionary' narrative.

20. Is 'The French Lieutenant's Woman' the right title for this novel? Why? Why not?

Contexts, comparisons and complementary readings

THE FRENCH LIEUTENANT'S WOMAN

These sections suggest contextual and comparative ways of reading these three novels by Fowles. You can put your reading in a social, historical or literary context. You can make comparisons – again, social, literary or historical – with other texts or art works. Or you can choose complementary works (of whatever kind) – that is, art works, literary works, social reportage or facts which in some way illuminate the text by sidelights or interventions which you can make into a telling framework. Some of the suggested contexts are directly connected to the book, in that they will give you precise literary or social frames in which to situate the novel. In turn, these are either related to the period within which the novel is set, or to the time – now – when you are reading it. Some of these examples are designed to suggest books or other texts that may make useful sources for comparison (or for complementary purposes) when you are reading *The Collector*, *The Magus* and *The French Lieutenant's Woman*. Again, they may be related to literary or critical themes, or they may be relevant to social and cultural themes current 'then' or 'now'.

Focus on: historical context

RESEARCH . . .

— 'The 1860s were in my opinion a crisis period in English history. The twentieth century really began in the 1860s.' Research the historical context of the 1860s. You might refer to E. Royston Pike's *Golden Times: Human Documents of the Victorian Age* (1967), which Fowles himself used, and which he describes as 'the best of all anthologies about the nineteenth century'. Alternatively, turn to *Mayhew's London* edited by Peter Quennell (1949), or – if you can get access to them – copies of *Punch* from the 1860s, from which Fowles gleaned details about food, clothes and dialogue.

Focus on: writing as an organic process

REWRITE . . .

— Fowles has described writing as an organic process: he has no idea where a novel is going when he starts. *The French Lieutenant's Woman* started in his mind with the image of a woman staring out to sea on the Cobb at Lyme Regis with her back turned. 'It was something to do with a woman being rejected and then in some way rejecting a man.' He does not plan his plots, but develops them from the inside. He has likened writing to plant-growing – a process of nurturing – and also to rambling: 'I always think the notion of the fork in the road is very important when you are creating narrative, because you are continually coming to forks. Now, if you write to an elaborate, pre-prepared plan, the choice is taken out of your hands . . . I like, in the actual business of writing, this feeling that you do not know where you are going.' Pick a moment in *The French Lieutenant's Woman* where a character takes a 'fork in the road' and rewrite the scenes following that decision or action as if he or she had taken another fork. As you write, adopt Fowles's technique of writing your narrative from the inside, not planning what will happen next until the moment of decision faces your characters. Does this process reveal anything to you about the process of creating narrative?

Focus on: the feminine principle

CONSIDER AND DISCUSS . . .

— Fowles was influenced by Jung's notion of the 'anima' or feminine principle, an archetype in the collective unconscious which is projected on to experience. He has said that his female characters 'are usually standing for other things. Women enshrine right feeling; a comprehensiveness of reaction to the world. Reason and right feeling are not the same thing.' How helpful do you find these comments in your interpretation of Fowles's female characters?

READ FURTHER . . .

— Fowles has often said that he has 'a feminine mind – creative, not logical'. He almost believes in the idea of the artist's muse, another projection of the anima, but finds it 'extremely naughty and unhelpful a lot of the time'. Moreover, he interprets his interest in the anima as part of his love of mystery, as if it were a ghost lying behind one's outward persona, even in men. Fowles has written a critique of Hardy's novel *The Well-Beloved* (1892), entitled 'Hardy and the Hag', which interprets that novel as a fable on the power of the anima in the life of the writer. In particular, he interprets the male character's pursuit of an idealised woman as the novelist's search to re-establish the son–mother bond. Read it for a fuller understanding of Fowles's ideas about the role of the anima in the novelist's art.

Focus on: dialogue and silence

CONJECTURE AND REFLECTION . . .

— Pay particular attention to the silences that punctuate Fowles's text, whether in the dialogue or in the gaps in the narrative, in what is not explained. 'I'm a deep believer in silence – the positive role of the negative. It can certainly be an obvious way to oblige the reader to help form and to experience the text.' Choose a moment of 'silence' in *The French Lieutenant's Woman* and consider what is not being said at that point in the dialogue or narrative. Then reflect on the effect of Fowles's use of silence at that point.

Focus on: freedom from convention

COMPARE . . .

— Fowles has always broken moulds and tried new narrative forms. 'Disbelieving set form is how I feel free,' he has said. How does this notion of freedom from literary conventions relate to the theme of breaking free from social conventions in *The French Lieutenant's Woman*?

Focus on: film adaptation

COMPARE MEDIA . . .

— The 1981 adaptation of *The French Lieutenant's Woman* (starring Meryl Streep and Jeremy Irons, with a screenplay by Harold Pinter) is the only adaptation of his novels that Fowles has said he likes. However, he has always voiced reservations about the way that cinema takes away the audience's power to imagine and supplies every detail for them. 'I sincerely admire Meryl Streep's performance in *The French Lieutenant's Woman*, but I am not so happy that she – or anyone who might have played the part – must present a fixed image for the subsequent reader. This mobility or fluidity of image, in terms of how readers "see" the text, is a very important asset of the novel.' On the other hand, he recognises the cinematic qualities of his fiction, and acknowledges that he has picked up useful techniques from cinema. Consider how cinema and literary fiction communicate similarly and how they communicate differently, and extend your consideration to an analysis of whether a film adaptation of a novel can ever truly represent the original. For a fuller account of the adaptation of the novel for the screen, you might refer to Fowles's article for *Vogue* (November 1981), 'Book to Movie: *The French Lieutenant's Woman*'.

Focus on: the Victorian novel

RESEARCH AND COMPARE . . .

— While Fowles's novel is a fiction in its own right, his technique includes a reflection on the modes and the methods of the classic Realist novel of the nineteenth century. No one novel is the precursor to his, but there are allusions and references that help to suggest backgrounds to *The French Lieutenant's Woman*. These might include: the idea of the unobtainable aloof woman in Charles Dickens's *Great Expectations* (1861); the independent governess in Charlotte Brontë's *Jane Eyre* (1847); the female adventurer in William Makepeace Thackeray's *Vanity Fair* (1847–8); Lyme Regis in Jane Austen's *Persuasion* (1818); class conflict and sexual exploitation in George Eliot's *Adam Bede* (1859) or Thomas Hardy's *Tess of the D'Urbervilles* (1891); science and evolutionary narratives in George Meredith's *The Egoist* (1879.)

Reference

Selected extracts from critical writings

These brief extracts from critical articles on John Fowles's work are designed to be used to suggest angles on the text that may be relevant to the themes of the books, their settings, their literary methods, their historical contexts, or to indicate their relevance to issues, questions or problems today.

Sometimes one critic's opinion will be entirely contradicted by another's. You might use these passages to ask yourself whether or not you agree with the writers' assessments. Or else you might take phrases from these articles to use for framing questions – for discussion, or for essays – about the texts.

None of these critical opinions are the last word. They are simply contributions to a cultural debate. As such, they should be approached with intellectual interest and intelligent assessment. But in the end, it is your own reading of a text that really counts.

Katherine Tarbox
From *The Art of John Fowles* (1988), p. 2
On Fowles's protagonists and plot structures

All the novels are the same story at bottom . . .
They begin with a protagonist who suffers some
degree of narcissism. He (or in the case of *The
Collector* and *A Maggot*, she) has been living an inauthentic life and playing roles that substitute for
true identity. He lives, as Nicholas might say, as
though someone were looking over his shoulder.
Nicholas Urfe sees himself as the *homme révolté*, while
Miranda see herself as the *femme révoltée*. Charles
Smithson tries to be a proper Victorian gentleman
. . . The protagonists are, however, in a state of dis-
equilibrium. They feel nebulously ill at ease in their
inauthentic lives, but do not know why; in fact, they
are not even aware that they are playing roles. They
are, to use one of Fowles's favorite metaphors,
schizophrenic – torn between what they perceive is
expected of them and what they dimly intuit they
need to be. Nicholas confesses, 'I was not the
person I wanted to be.'

Katherine Tarbox
From *The Art of John Fowles* (1988), pp. 9–10
On the attitude and approach that Fowles's novels
demand from the reader

I approach the novels on Fowles's own terms, which
demand that the reader first submit to the Godgame,
then step back and see the experience whole. I have
tried to communicate the real pleasure of coming to

understand his work, a kind of *jouissance* that matches the spirit of the novels themselves. The novels are participatory fictions, and because they deal with the education of each individual reader, critical analyses must always be largely personal. But much of what Fowles has to say may also be enjoyed communally. It is for all these reasons that my essays suggest a *way* in which to read these diffi-cult novels. The voice I have adopted, that is, of critic-as-authority, is more a sacrifice to convention than any conviction of omniscience which, in any event, Fowles will quickly dispel. These essays are intended to be heuristic, in keeping with the philos-ophy their subjects so elegantly expound.

William J. Palmer
From *The Fiction of John Fowles: Tradition, Art, and the Loneliness of Selfhood* (1974), pp. 1–2
On Fowles's playful worlds

Fowles's fiction is like a huge protean amusement park, a literary Disney World enisled in a sea of potential interpretation. But the park is sinister, not gay; dark, not ferris-wheel-lighted and lantern-strung. And the people who come to the park are always alone. They pass through the main gate where Dostoevsky, a microphoned Cerberus, barks, 'Step right inside, everything is permitted!' Sartre sells tickets to the maze and Camus operates the lightless ferris wheel which never stops yet progresses. Richardson shows people into the inner darkness where the girlie show bumps and grinds in the night, and Conrad mans the turnstile to jungle land.

Dickens and Hardy, uniformed men to be respected, patrol the midway and enforce the rules. Unlike most amusement parks, however, in the Fowles world illusion becomes reality rather than vice versa.

William J. Palmer
From *The Fiction of John Fowles: Tradition, Art, and the Loneliness of Selfhood* (1974), p. 3
On the idea of 'reflection' in Fowles's novels

As the novelist's intrusions into *The French Lieutenant's Woman* and the very existence of *The Aristos* testify, Fowles is a writer stalking himself. Or better, he is a novelist writing into a mirror so that each of his works reflects back upon his own mind and vision.

Barbara McKenzie
From *The Process of Fiction* (1969), pp. 10–11
On the intervention and the narrative method

The manoeuverings, transitional assists, and interpretive comments of the privileged narrator frequently break the illusion of reality engendered by the people and action he is depicting. At such times, the machinery of narration calls attention to itself and to the story as artifice – an effect only occasionally described as a narrative technique.

Susana Onega
From *Form and Meaning in the Novels of
John Fowles* (1989), p. 10
On freedom and Fowles's narrative method

Fowles's yearning for absolute creative liberty reflects,
in mirror image, his fictional hero's struggle for
freedom and echoes the fear of determinism felt by
the existentialist. Thus, in a nutshell, Fowles metaphorically synthesizes the thematic core of his obsessive
rewriting. By writing symphonic variations of the only
conceivable situation – a fiction hero's quest for
maturity and freedom – Fowles is telling us that even
if liberty proves to be unattainable, it is at least possible to create the illusion of this freedom. But we
should not forget that, as we learn from the reading
of his novels, for Fowles reality and unreality, the
ontological and the fictional, enjoy the same status.

Liz-Anne Bawden, Kevin Padian and
Hugh S. Torrens
From 'The Undercliff of John Fowles's *The French
Lieutenant's Woman*: A Note on Geology, and
Geography', in James R. Aubrey, ed., *John Fowles and
Nature: Fourteen Perspectives on Landscape* (1999), p. 151
On nature and the natural world

An acute sensitivity to nature is a central characteristic of John Fowles's writing. Ancient history, as
well as the human history of a region, is a recurring
motif in the novels, from *The Magus* and *The French
Lieutenant's Woman* onward, and 'natural history', in
the best sense of the term, is a principal focus of

much of his later work. He uses nature for many literary purposes: the great age of the rocks of the Undercliff, with the gigantic hiatus in time between their upper and lower reaches; the harbinger of the past as well as the future, the peculiar wilderness of the Undercliff, with its promise of freedom in contrast to the iron-bound constraints of Mrs Poulteney's drawing room. The erotic effects of its beauty and its seclusion lend an almost palpable excitement to Charles's meetings there with Sarah.

Jan Relf, ed.,
From 'Introduction' to *Wormholes: Essays and Occasional Writings* (1998), p. xii
On Fowles's key themes

The writer's obsessions and passions permeate his work, and readers who are familiar with Fowles's novels will find in these essays frequent resonances and reflections of themes that they may already have met in the fiction: the lost *domaine*; the woman as *princesse lointaine*; evolution and natural history; freedom and responsibility; randomness and hazard; literature, literariness, and the role of the writer. They also reflect his lifelong commitment to left-wing politics, conservation, and 'green' issues. And the gift for narrative, for which Fowles's novels are so justly celebrated, is evident in many of these essays. In 'Shipwreck', for instance, the opening lines have all the qualities of a compelling story: the feeling of 'once upon a time', the powerful sense of place, and the way the first-person narrator draws the reader into the here and now of the tale he is telling.

Glossary of literary terms

Allusion A conscious reference to some other text, idea, art object or historical fact, which is designed to cast light on the situation under discussion.

Analepsis A narrative 'flashback' in time.

Anima/animus In terms of the philosophy of Jung, a reference to the unconscious traits that we hide even from ourselves, whether 'feminine' – the 'anima', which is kind, caring, nurturing and feeling – or 'masculine', the 'animus', which is aggressive, self-interested, determined and self-motivated.

Archetype Any idea or story that has spawned many other ideas and stories that have since become absorbed – at both conscious and unconscious levels – into the culture. Examples might include the Cinderella story. Think about how this 'archetype' connects to the real-life facts of the marriage between the Prince of Wales and Diana Spencer.

Authentic/authenticity In existentialism – a philosophical position which holds that the universe has no intrinsic meaning or purpose and no fixed system of values, and therefore that people must create their essential natures by exercising their complete freedom of choice about their actions – authenticity means making those choices freely, resisting social pressures and escaping the fetters of conventional morality.

Bricolage The improvised ordering of the minutiae of the physical world into structures which have a logic of their own, by which 'nature' and 'culture' are made to mirror each other.

Cliché From the French 'to cut'. The key idea is that a 'cliché' no longer has a viable 'cutting' edge.

Collage In literature, an experimental and intertextual narrative strategy, containing a mixture of references, quotations, allusions and foreign expressions.

Confession narrative A story – a narrative – which is couched in terms of a self-revelation, although this may be deceptive. That is, a first-person narrative, where the protagonist says, 'Yes. I did it.'

Darwinism Defining your life according to the philosophy and scientific principles of Charles Darwin. These are complex, and – for a short (ish!) version – the best thing is to read Philip Appleman's Norton edition of Darwin's key texts (1979). But essentially, in conventional Victorian shorthand, 'Darwinism' suggests a belief in evolution and natural selection as the principles of physical existence in the world, as opposed to a belief in the biblical version of Creation where God made the world in seven days.

Determinism A quasi-theological term much used in the nineteenth century and in relation to the classic nineteenth-century novel. It suggests – on the one hand – that all in life is 'determined' – whether by fate, or an all-powerful God. But it also suggests – on the other hand – that it is our own choices that govern what subsequently happens to us. Note this epigraph, composed by George Eliot for one of the chapter headings to her own novel *Adam Bede* (1859): 'Our deeds determine us, much as we determine our deeds.'

Didactic Telling you what to think, categorically.

Epigram A brief – and often witty – summary of a fact, idea, concept or picture.

Epistolary novel A novel written in letters, particularly popular in the eighteenth century. Examples include Samuel Richardson's *Clarissa* (1748–9) and Alice Walker's *The Color Purple* (1983).

Euphemism A phrase that means something different, more polite, than the thing to which it actually refers. In *Experience* (2000), for instance, Martin Amis tells the story of how his father was asked if he wished to 'wash his hands'. 'No thank you,' he replied, 'I washed them behind a bush on the way down.' No hands at all were washed of course.

Existentialism A philosophical position which holds that in a universe that has no intrinsic meaning or purpose and no fixed system of values, people have complete freedom of choice about their actions, must create their essential natures by exercising that freedom, and must accept complete responsibility for their actions. Sartre's maxim, 'Existence precedes essence', sums it up succinctly.

Fable From the Old French '*fabliaux*'. A short, pithy, inventive story which has some kind of moral, but probably entertains as well.

Fairy tales Originally folk tales, and part of the oral tradition, first recorded in the early nineteenth century by the brothers Grimm. Key ingredients are: disguises, charms, magic, spells, and a hero and a heroine who enjoy adventures and endure difficulties before living happily ever after.

Feminist Not a single ideology, but a plurality of perspectives on the origin and the constitution of gender, sexuality, male power structures and female emancipation. 'I myself have never been able to find out precisely what feminism is: I only know that people call me a feminist whenever I express sentiments that differentiate me from a doormat or a prostitute' (Rebecca West, 1892–1983).

Fragmentation A non-realist narrative strategy that values the privileging of small, broken-off pieces over the whole, monumental work of art.

Gothic novel A literary development dating from the late eighteenth century. Key ingredients are: secrets, sexual threat, caves, locked rooms, hidden places, the occult, ruins, fragments, extravagance, the dark, the perverted, the witchy.

Idyll Like Pastoral, an episode or scene of rural life, usually serene and idealised. A form of nostalgia for lost innocence by urban writers.

Magus/magi Originally, a caste of priest with occult powers, derived from the ancient Brahmins of India. In folklore and literature, one who possesses magical powers over people, nature and the spirit world through the study of esoteric knowledge and the liberal arts.

Marxist theory A development of literary criticism that bases itself on the terms of the theories of Karl Marx and Friedrich Engels as expressed in their *Communist Manifesto* (1848). In its most simplistic form, it means paying attention to the deprived, the dispossessed and the degraded in any text.

Masque Originally, a dance involving figures wearing masks. By the sixteenth century, an elaborate and increasingly splendid form of courtly entertainment, comprising music, song, dancing, drama and (one supposes) intrigue. The ironies that 'disguising' provides have long been employed by dramatists.

Metafiction From the Greek, meaning above, or beyond, fiction. In literary theory, metafiction refers to the act of commenting on (and therefore revealing) the processes of fiction-making even while practising them.

Motif From a musical category. A 'motif' is a signature theme (in music) or a word, or an idea, that always represents a specific person, scene, theme or idea.

Muse A person (usually) but also an idea, a concept, a theme, a mood that inspires the author – any author. In terms of Greek myth there were Nine Muses, the acolytes of Apollo, god of music and poetry.

Nymph A minor female divinity of classical mythology.

Parable A short, allegorical story that illustrates a moral lesson.

Parody Where a serious text is questioned by an imitation that makes it comic.

Pastiche A self-conscious and artful version of the above.

Pensée A thought or a reflection, specifically one expressed in literary form. It may possess the brevity of an aphorism, or proliferate to many pages.

Quest narrative A story where the hero is looking for something, often the answer to a question or the tracking down of an idealised object. In fact, most quest narratives are about the search for the self. 'To avoid discovery I stay on the run. To discover things for myself I stay on the run' (Jeanette Winterson, *The PowerBook*, 2000).

Realism The presentation of the 'real' as opposed to 'fantasy' or 'ideal'. Television soap operas are supposed to be 'realist' in that they are true to life.

Romance Connected to the medieval concept of romance where an admired lady or *princesse lointaine* – faraway princess – is the object of an idealised love.

Satyr A minor woodland deity, a lecherous mix of horse and goat, and a regular at Dionysian revels.

Self-reflexivity A non-realist narrative strategy in which the narrative is primarily concerned with its own interests – commentary, that is, on fiction in fiction.

Sympathy Emotional identification with a person or with a literary character – 'feeling with'.

Thriller Anything designed to have a 'thrilling' effect on the reader.

Biographical outline

1926 Born 31 March in Leigh-on-Sea, to Robert J. Fowles and Gladys Richards.

1944 Attended the University of Edinburgh for six months.

1945–6 Served as a lieutenant in the Royal Marines.

1947–50 Studied French at New College, Oxford.

1950–1 Lecturer in English at the University of Poitiers, France.

1951–2 Taught English at Anargyrios College, in Spetsai, Greece.

1953–63 Held various teaching posts in and around London, eventually as head of English at St Godric's, Hampstead.

1963 *The Collector* published.

1964 *The Aristos: A Self-Portrait in Ideas* published.

1965 *The Magus* published in America. Film of *The Collector* released. Settled in Lyme Regis.

1966 *The Magus* published in Britain.

1968 Revised edition of *The Aristos* published. Film of *The Magus* released.

1969 *The French Lieutenant's Woman* published. Wins the Silver Pen Award from the English Centre of PEN.

1970 Wins the W.H. Smith & Son Award.

1973 *Poems* published.

1974 *The Ebony Tower* published.

1977 Revised edition of *The Magus* published in Britain (appears in America in 1978). *Daniel Martin* published. Translates Molière's *Don Juan* (1665) and Alfred de Musset's *Lorenzaccio* (1834) for the National Theatre, London. Publishes a translation of Claire de Duras's novel *Ourika* (1824).

1978 *Islands* published, with photographs by Fay Godwin.

1979 *The Tree* published.

1980 *The Enigma of Stonehenge* published.

1981 Film of *The French Lieutenant's Woman*, directed by Karel Reisz with a screenplay by Harold Pinter, released.

1982 *Mantissa* published.

1985 *A Maggot* published.

1988 *Wormholes: Essays and Occasional Writings* published.

2003/4 *Journals* Vols. I and II published.

Select bibliography

WORKS BY JOHN FOWLES

The Collector (Jonathan Cape, London, 1963; Vintage, London, 1998)

The Aristos: A Self-Portrait in Ideas (Jonathan Cape, 1964; Vintage, 2001)

The Magus (Jonathan Cape, 1966; Vintage, 1997)

The French Lieutenant's Woman (Jonathan Cape 1969; Vintage, 1996)

Poems (Ecco Press, New York, 1973)

The Ebony Tower (Jonathan Cape, 1974; Vintage, 1997)

Shipwreck, text by Fowles with photographs by the Gibsons of Scilly (Jonathan Cape, 1974)

Daniel Martin (Jonathan Cape, 1977; Vintage, 1998)

Islands, text by Fowles with photographs by Fay Godwin (Jonathan Cape, 1978)

The Tree (Jonathan Cape, 1979; Vintage, 2000)

The Enigma of Stonehenge, text by Fowles with photographs by Barry Brukoff (Jonathan Cape, 1980)

Mantissa (Jonathan Cape, 1982)

A Short History of Lyme Regis (Little Brown, Boston, 1982)

A Maggot (Jonathan Cape, 1985; Vintage, 1996)

Lyme Regis Camera (Little Brown, 1990)

Wormholes: Essays and Occasional Writings (Jonathan Cape, 1988; Vintage, 1999)

OTHER WORKS

'I Write Therefore I Am', *Evergreen Review*, 8 (August–September 1964)

'Notes on an Unfinished Novel', in *Afterwords: Novelists on Their Novels*, ed. Thomas McCormack (Harper & Row, New York, 1969)

'Hardy and the Hag', in *Thomas Hardy After Fifty Years*, ed. Lance St John Butler (Macmillan, London, 1977)

'Book to Movie: *The French Lieutenant's Woman*', *Vogue* (November 1981)

Henri Alain-Fournier, *Les Grands Meaulnes*, translated as *The Wanderer*, afterword by John Fowles (American Library, New York, 1971)

Claire de Duras, *Ourika* (1824), translated, with an introduction and epilogue, by John Fowles (W. Thomas Taylor, Austin, Texas, 1977)

Many of Fowles's most important essays and previously uncollected writings are included in *Wormholes: Essays and Occasional Writings*. Among them 'I Write Therefore I Am' (1964), 'Greece' (1996), 'On Being English but not British' (1964), 'Weeds, Bugs and Americans' (1970), 'Islands' (1978), and 'The Nature of Nature' (1995). It also includes an interview with Dianne L. Vipond from 1996.

CRITICAL WORKS

James Acheson, *John Fowles* (Macmillan Modern Novelist series, New York, 1998). A very brief but useful summary of the main themes in the major novels.

James R. Aubrey, *John Fowles: A Reference Companion* (Greenwood Press, Westport, Connecticut, 1991). Chapters on Fowles's life, on his non-fiction, brief accounts of the plots of the fiction, a chapter on critical approaches to the fiction – the most useful section of the book – notes on the allusions in the fictions, a census of characters in the novels and a helpful bibliography.

James R. Aubrey, ed., *John Fowles and Nature: Fourteen Perspectives on Landscape* (Associated Press, London, 1999). Includes an afterword by John Fowles; excellent essays on islands and 'narrative's negative space' by Katherine Tarbox; on the archetype of the green man by Barry N. Olshen; on evolutionary legacy and Darwinian landscapes in *The French Lieutenant's Woman* by Kevin Padian; and on Greek myths and legends in *The Magus* by Kirke Kefalea.

Tamás Bényei, *Acts of Attention: Figure and Narrative in Postwar British Novels* (Peter Lang, Frankfurt am Main, 1999). Includes a chapter entitled 'Seduction and the Politics of Reading in *The French Lieutenant's Woman*', which deals with the themes of 'Victorian Mimicry and the Parables of Authority', 'Narrative Seduction' and 'Confession' (pp. 65–91). This chapter sets the novel up as 'a key text of a peculiarly British brand of postmodernism' and deals intelligently with the three narrative strategies of imitation, the seduction of the reader and the mode of confession.

Malcolm Bradbury, 'The Novelist as Impresario: The Fiction of John Fowles', in *No, Not Bloomsbury* (Columbia University Press, New York, 1988), pp. 279–93.

Jerome Bump, 'The Narrator as Proto-reader in *The French Lieutenant's Woman*', *Victorian Newsletter*, 74 (Fall 1988), pp. 16–18.

Robert Burden, *John Fowles, John Hawkes, Claude Simon: Problems of Self and Form in the Post-Modernist Novel: A Comparative Study* (Konigshausen and Neumann, Wurzburg, 1980). A postgraduate thesis which never escapes its origins. All you need to know is that it deals with three issues: the idea of identity and the construction of the self; narrative structure; parody and pastiche and the manipulation of the reader's expectations.

Deborah Byrd, 'The Evolution and Emancipation of Sarah

Woodruff: *The French Lieutenant's Woman* as a Feminist Novel', in *International Journal of Women's Studies*, 7 (1984), pp. 306–21.

Peter Conradi, *John Fowles* (Methuen, London and New York, 1982). A short and straightforward summary of Fowles's work up to *Daniel Martin*, taking the premise that Fowles's novels can be read as 'modern romances'.

Joanne V. Creighton, 'The Reader and Modern and Post-Modern Fiction', in *College Literature*, 9 (1982), pp. 216–30.

Bo H. T. Eriksson, *The 'Structuring Forces' of Detection: The Cases of C. P. Snow and John Fowles* (Uppsala, 1995). A doctoral thesis that focuses on the idea of mystery and the structures of detective fiction as the key shape in the works of Fowles. Includes a chapter on *The Collector*, one on *The Ebony Tower* and one on the three major novels, *The Magus*, *The French Lieutenant's Woman* and *Daniel Martin*.

Pamela Faber and Celia Wallhead, 'The Lexical Field of Visual Perception in *The French Lieutenant's Woman* by John Fowles', in 4:2, *Language and Literature* (1995), pp. 127–44.

Harald William Fawkner, *The Timescapes of John Fowles* (Associated University Presses, London and Toronto, 1984). Eschewing the usual account of 'influences', Hawkner tackles a subject that Fowles says – in a specially written foreword for this critical book – 'particularly interests me personally'. As Fowles notes in a letter he sent to the critic, 'Fiction-writing is an intrinsically diachronic business, using the word in its linguistics sense: only to be undertaken and analysed that way.' Issues dealt with here include 'Space-time and Reality', 'Pasts' and 'Time Schemes'.

Charles Garard, *Point of View in Fiction and Film: Focus on John Fowles* (Peter Lang, Frankfurt am Main and New York, 1991). A helpful and succinct account comparing and contrasting the film adaptations of *The Collector*, *The Magus* and *The French Lieutenant's Woman*. A very helpful account of the translation of novel to cinema screen. Particularly good on comparisons and analogies with other films, including Hitchcock's *Vertigo* and Alain Resnais's *Hiroshima, Mon Amour* and *Last Year at Marienbad*.

David Gross, 'Historical Consciousness and the Modern Novel: The Uses of History in the Fiction of John Fowles', *Studies in the Humanities*, 7.1 (1978), pp. 19–27.

Constance B. Hieatt, '*Eliduc* Revisited: John Fowles and Marie de France', in *English Studies in Canada*, 3 (1977), pp. 351–8.

Robert Huffaker, *John Fowles* (Twayne Publishers, G. K. Hall, Boston, Mass., 1980). Deals with the two versions of *The Magus*. Includes a brief summary of the Jungian elements and the roles of ritual, symbol and myth. Sections on *The French Lieutenant's Woman* deal with the intrusive narrator, the notion of the historical novel and the theme of evolution.

Linda Hutcheon, 'The "Real World(s)" of Fiction: *The French Lieutenant's Woman*', in *English Studies in Canada*, 4 (1978), pp. 81–94.

Tatjana Jukic, 'From Worlds to Words and the Other Way Around: The Victorian Inheritance in the Postmodern British Novel', in Richard Todd and Luisa Flora, eds, *Theme Parks, Rainforests, and Sprouting Wastelands: European Essays on Theory and Performance in Contemporary British Fiction* (Rodopi, Amsterdam, 2000), pp. 77–87.

Richard C. Kane, *Iris Murdoch, Muriel Spark, and John Fowles: Didactic Demons in Modern Fiction* (Associated University Presses, London and Toronto, 1988). Chapters on the enclosed world of *The Collector* and on *The Magus* as 'Greek Gothic'.

David W. Landrum, 'Sarah and Sappho: Lesbian Reference in *The French Lieutenant's Woman*', 33 (1), *Mosaic* (2000), pp. 59–76. The treatment of Sarah and her relationship to the Pre-Raphaelites.

Rebecca Lin, 'Medusa, Siren or Sphinx: Retrieving the Female Gaze and Voice in *The French Lieutenant's Woman*', 8

December, *Sl & LT* (1998), pp. 199–213. Compares the imaging of the female gaze in Fowles, with that presented in Joseph Conrad's *The Heart of Darkness*.

Simon Loveday, *The Romances of John Fowles* (Macmillan, London and Basingstoke, 1985). A chapter on the 'life and work' and then chapters on all the major novels up to *Daniel Martin*. Uncomplicated summaries of what the critic considers to be Fowles's four main themes: the Few and the Many; the *domaine*; the contrast between masculine and feminine mentality; and the difficult necessity of freedom. Includes a useful bibliography.

Terry Lovell, 'Feminism and Form in the Literary Adaptation: *The French Lieutenant's Woman*', in Jeremy Hawthorn, ed., *Criticism and Critical Theory* (Edwin Arnold, London, 1984), pp. 112–26.

John Neary, *Somethingness and Nothingness: The Fiction of John Updike and John Fowles* (Southern Illinois University Press, Carbondale and Edwardsville, 1992). Chapters include 'Rebellion and Repetition in *The Collector*', 'Self and the Other in *The Magus*', 'Sex as a Subversion in *The French Lieutenant's Woman*'.

Barry N. Olshen, *John Fowles* (Frederick Ungar Publishing Co., New York, 1978). A straightforward and brief account of the novels, including the three covered in this guide. Begins with a short biographical account of Fowles's writing.

Barry N. Olshen and Toni A. Olshen, *John Fowles: A Reference Guide* (G. K. Hall, Boston, Mass., 1980). A useful listing of Fowles's works to 1980, and criticism written about him from 1963 to 1979. It includes lists of stage and screen adaptations of his works, and lists of his poetry and short fictions as well as book reviews, essays, articles and miscellaneous non-fiction written by Fowles to 1979, among them an article on Jacqueline Onassis, on 'Is the Novel Dead?', and on other writers such as Thomas Hardy and Henri Alain-Fournier.

Fowles's wide range of interests and influences is displayed in these listings. The bibliography of critical writings on Fowles's work is annotated and includes brief summaries of contemporary reviews.

Susana Onega, *Form and Meaning in the Novels of John Fowles* (UMI Research Press, Ann Arbor and London, 1989). An impressive and theoretically sophisticated analysis of all the major books up to *A Maggot*. Includes a very useful interview with Fowles.

William J. Palmer, *The Fiction of John Fowles: Tradition, Art, and the Loneliness of Selfhood* (University of Missouri Press, Columbia, 1974). A sensible account of Fowles's relation to a variety of literary traditions and his exploitation of a self-consciously literary method.

Ellen Pifer, ed., *Critical Essays on John Fowles* (G. K. Hall, Boston, Mass., 1986).

Elizabeth D. Rankin, 'Cryptic Coloration in *The French Lieutenant's Woman*', in *Journal of Narrative Technique*, 3 (1974), pp. 193–207.

Jane E. Robison, 'Echoes of the Masque in *The Magus*', in *Publications of the Missouri Philological Association*, 21 (1996), pp. 77–82.

Barbara Rommerskirchen, *Constructing Reality: Constructivism and Narration in John Fowles's The Magus* (Peter Lang, Frankfurt am Main, 1999). An MA thesis which closely analyses the theme of constructivism and describes *The Magus* as a novel which is in process.

Gilbert J. Rose, '*The French Lieutenant's Woman*: The Unconscious Significance of a Novel to its Author', in *American Imago*, 29 (1972), pp. 165–76.

Roberta Rubinstein, 'Myth, Mystery and Irony: John Fowles's *The Magus*' in *Contemporary Literature*, 16 (Summer 1975), pp. 328–39.

Robert Scholes, 'The Orgiastic Fiction of John Fowles', in

Hollins Critic, 65 (1969), pp. 1–12. Reprinted, with revisions, in Robert Scholes, *Fabulation and Metafiction* (University of Illinois Press, Urbana, 1979), pp. 37–45.

Robert Siegle, 'Fowles, Contemporary Fiction and the Poetics of the Author', in *The Politics of Reflexivity: Narrative and the Constitutive Poetics of Culture* (Johns Hopkins University Press, Baltimore, 1986), pp. 169–261. Originally published as an article, 'The Concept of the Author in Barthes, Foucault and Fowles', in *College Literature*, 10.2 (1983), pp. 126–38.

Jason C. Smith, 'Schrödinger's Cat and Sarah's Child: John Fowles's Quantum Narrative', 32 (2), *Mosaic* (June, 1999), pp. 91–106.

Katherine Tarbox, *The Art of John Fowles* (University of Georgia Press, Athens and London, 1988). A persuasive account of Fowles's themes of identity, metamorphosis and 'the survival of individual freedom'.

Dianne L. Vipond, ed., *Conversations with John Fowles* (University of Mississippi Press, Jackson, 1999). An excellent collection of interviews ranging from 1963 to 1999.

Patricia Waugh, *Metafiction: The Theory and Practice of Self-Conscious Fiction* (Methuen, London and New York, 1984). Includes some discussion of *The French Lieutenant's Woman*.

Peter Wolfe, *John Fowles, Magus and Moralist* (Bucknell University Press Ltd, Lewisburg and London, 1976; revised edn 1979). A somewhat old-fashioned account of literary criticism mainly concentrating on *The Collector*, *The Magus* and *The French Lieutenant's Woman*. Wolfe takes Fowles's philosophical ideas and attempts to explain how he combines intellectual sophistication with popular appeal. But while he acknowledges Fowles as a literary writer, he deals less with the technical side and more with his function as a popular moralist.

Bruce Woodcock, *Male Mythologies: John Fowles and Masculinity*, (The Harvester Press, Brighton, Sussex, 1984). Focusing on *The Collector*, *The Magus*, *The French Lieutenant's Woman*, *Daniel*

Martin and *Mantissa*, this presents a reasoned and significant analysis of an important theme in Fowles's work. The chapter headings alone suggest the range and value of the work: from the theme of Bluebeard in *The Collector*, to the idea of the 'figure in the unconscious' in *The French Lieutenant's Woman*, and the focus on 'masculinity on trial' in *The Magus*. The chapter on *Mantissa* is entitled 'Men, will they ever grow up?' A discerning and fruitful analysis.

The editors

Jonathan Noakes has taught English in secondary schools in Britain and Australia for sixteen years. For six years he ran A-level English studies at Eton College where he is a housemaster.

Margaret Reynolds is Reader in English at Queen Mary, University of London, and the presenter of BBC Radio 4's *Adventures in Poetry*. Her publications include *The Sappho Companion* and (with Angela Leighton) *Victorian Women Poets*. Her most recent book is *The Sappho History*.